Why I

Bernard Bergonzi is Professor of English at the University of Warwick.

Mary Craig, writer and broadcaster, is the author of *Blessings* and *Man from a Far Country* (a biography of Pope John Paul II).

Clifford Longley is Religious Affairs Correspondent of *The Times*.

James Mackey is Thomas Chalmers Professor of Theology in the University of Edinburgh.

Louis McRedmond is a journalist and writer living in Dublin.

Robert Nowell, writer and journalist, is the author of *A Passion for Truth*.

Piers Paul Read is a novelist and critic.

Also by Robert Nowell

A Passion for Truth: Hans Küng – A Biography (Collins)

WHY I AM STILL A CATHOLIC

Bernard Bergonzi, Mary Craig,
Clifford Longley, James Mackey,
Louis McRedmond and Piers Paul Read

edited by Robert Nowell

Collins
FOUNT PAPERBACKS

First published by William Collins Sons & Co Ltd, Glasgow, 1982
Published by Fount Paperbacks, London, 1983

Made and printed in Great Britain by
William Collins Sons & Co Ltd, Glasgow

Contents

Growth into Freedom

ROBERT NOWELL

1

Growth into Freedom

ROBERT NOWELL

BEING A CATHOLIC is something that, to the outward eye at least, has changed rather dramatically within our lifetime. Thirty years ago Catholics worshipped in a dead language, abstained from meat on Fridays, went regularly to confession, refused to use contraceptives, and were very nervous about disagreeing with each other and above all with official Church teaching on a wide range of issues regarded as central to their faith. Today the Mass is in English, Friday abstinence has gone, the Saturday night queue outside the confessional is no more, most married Catholics use contraceptives, and freedom of speech within the Church is taken for granted – at least by the laity.

Of these changes the most fundamental is the rediscovery of freedom. The example was set by the Second Vatican Council, when over a period of four years two thousand bishops from all over the world debated publicly in St Peter's, Rome, questions that ordinary Catholics had been encouraged to believe were not open to debate. The lesson was confirmed when, in 1968, Paul VI re-affirmed the Church's traditional condemnation of 'artificial' methods of birth control after a period of open debate had encouraged Catholics to look forward to change and made it difficult, if not impossible, for them to accept the old teaching with any conviction.

In these circumstances being a Catholic can paradoxically appear more difficult. It is no longer (if it ever was) a question of simply accepting some ready-made formula. Less and less can one rely on the tribal cohesiveness of the Catholic community: even in Ireland there are signs that the social cohesion which has helped to maintain a society in which ninety per cent of Catholics go to Sunday Mass is beginning to crumble. Being a Catholic has more and more become a matter of explicit personal conviction, something that the individual Catholic has to work out for himself or herself in terms of his or her own life. And often enough the outcome can diverge fairly radically from what the official Church regards as entailed by being a Catholic. What would from official pronouncements seem important can appear less so to the individual believer, and *vice versa*. These are no doubt necessary and unavoidable tensions, but they are emphasised by the temper of the present pontificate, and no doubt will be thrown into sharp relief by the visit to Britain of Pope John Paul II in May 1982.

In the essays which make up this volume seven of us explore how and why and to what extent we remain Catholics in a Church which has altered considerably from that in which we were brought up or which we joined. Between us we present a fair cross-section of the Catholic community in these islands. Two are Irishmen: one, Louis McRedmond, living and working in Dublin, the other, James P. Mackay, a 'laicised priest' (whatever that contradiction in terms may mean) who is now Thomas Chalmers Professor of Theology at Edinburgh. Two of us are converts: myself and Clifford Longley, religious affairs correspondent of *The Times*, who as readers will see steadfastly resists any attempt to stick labels on him. The other three are all, in English parlance, cradle Catholics: the writer and broadcaster Mary Craig, brought up in the heartland of English Catholicism; the critic and novelist Bernard Bergonzi, who grew up in the Catholic diaspora of south London; and the novelist Piers Paul Read, brought up a Catholic by a mother barred from the sacraments. The range of response is, I think, at least as wide as the diversity of backgrounds. Among other things it shows the risks inherent in trying to predict somebody's views from the mere fact that he or she is known to be a Catholic, or the dangers of attempting to classify Catholics under labels such as 'conservative' or 'progressive'. Some of what might be thought to be the most 'conservative' traits are to be found in James Mackey, yet at the same time some of the most radical. Perhaps it is no accident that he is the professional theologian amongst us.

A certain comprehensiveness would thus seem now to have become an integral aspect of Catholicism. Perhaps it always was, but in the pre-conciliar Church it was rather effectively buried beneath the strong emphasis on verbal orthodoxy and the intolerance of deviation that marked Catholicism up till the accession of John XXIII. This raises the question whether the present climate of toleration has been merely a brief inter-glacial period, with episodes like the disciplining of Hans Küng and the interrogation of Edward Schillebeeckx foreshadowing a return of the ice-sheet of conformity to a rigid standard imposed more or less arbitrarily by Rome, or whether some irreversible change has taken place in the Catholic mentality akin to that which makes everyone in the western world far less patient of authority than they were a generation ago. The hope must be that the Church as a whole is now secure enough in its belief not simply to tolerate but actively to encourage all its members to think about what they believe as an essential part of ensuring that it is what they *themselves* believe.

The mention of comprehensiveness, and the disappearance of those distinctive practices like Latin in the liturgy that marked Catholics off from other Christians, could encourage the view – in England, but not of course in Ireland – that Catholicism is simply becoming assimilated to the pattern of institutional Christianity represented by the Church of England and, to some extent, the Free Churches. In that case, why should not a convert like myself anticipate the outcome of all these years of ecumenical endeavour, with doctrinal agreement found to exist in areas where it had been thought impossible, and find a comfortable niche within Anglicanism or make my home in the Nonconformist tradition of prophetic independence?

But the whole ecumenical movement could simply be regarded as the huddling together of Churches that have steadily been losing both influence and members. In England the great majority of people have found that they can get on very well without much in the way of any formal link with institutional religion. Being a Christian can thus appear simply a gesture of piety towards the past out of which we have grown and which, we sometimes like to think, we have grown out of. Behind the question why I am still a Catholic thus lurks the question why I am a Christian in the first place.

Christianity, after all, can seem to demand beliefs that flout common sense and contradict the assumptions on which we base our lives. The simplest way of reading the story recounted in the gospels for many people is to take it literally: virgin birth, miracles, the resurrection itself in the sense of a corpse restored to tangible, physical life. On this understanding there is a supernatural element which from time to time intervenes in and radically affects the natural fabric of our lives. There are many Christians who can only live on this basis, as it were as citizens of two worlds, this world and a supernatural other world that has already broken in on the natural world we inhabit. Piers Paul Read in this book in fact decries efforts to explain away the supernatural element in Christianity and sees them as undermining the essential coherence of the gospel.

Yet for many others the supernatural element presents an insuperable obstacle. It represents a retreat into the world of fairy-tale rather than an attempt to grapple with the grim realities of life and above all of death. For me, the reality of the other dimension which the gospel points to and opens up for us is trivialised by thinking of it in terms of a sphere of causation over and above the flux of causation underlying the world in which I live, as if God were some master magician. I am prepared to accept that there is a coherent natural explanation underlying all the apparently miraculous events recorded in the gospels, even perhaps the resurrection. What is 'supernatural' about them is what they mean, is the interpretation we as Christians have come to see must be put on them, just as the people of Israel came to see God supremely at work in their deliverance from bondage in Egypt. In this way the gospel recounts God at work saving and delivering his people; but to read it in this way requires that mysterious response we call faith. The evidence is not compelling in the way that mathematical proof or experimental demonstration is compelling.

I suspect I am not alone in finding that I have gradually drifted towards this understanding of the supernatural element in Christianity. There were no great pressures to force me to reconcile my understanding of the world in terms of modern science and my understanding of it as a Christian. But slowly the two became reconciled, and I realised that being a Catholic did not necessarily mean, for example, having to accept the virgin birth as a physical reality.

All this is rather a grey area where Church authority can be reluctant to intervene and, when it does, is apt to make rather a fool of itself. It is noteworthy, for example, that in its harrying of Küng and Schillebeeckx the Doctrinal Congregation in Rome did not make an issue of the virgin birth, no doubt fully aware that if it did it would have the ground cut from under its feet by the majority of Catholic scripture scholars. Yet it is here, perhaps, that the line of division runs within the Churches, between those who adopt a more literal interpretation of the gospels and the creeds and those who attempt an interpretation that does justice to the claims of both faith and reason without reducing Christianity merely to the story of a remarkable man. It is a division that can cause a great deal of trouble, because of the tacit assumptions each side has about what their faith demands of them: either 'you *can't* believe that in that sense' or 'but you *must* believe this in this way'. The temptation is for each side to want somehow to un-Church. Yet what unites them is surely more important: a common belief in an underlying and over-arching reality that offers the ultimate promise of making sense of the tantalisingly ambiguous world in which we live.

It is here that I find Christianity essential with its assurance that the world is essentially good and that in some mysterious way it is moving towards some ultimate and unimaginable fulfilment. It is here, surely, and not over the details of the gospel story, that Christianity demands the seemingly impossible. Even the natural world may at times seem benign, yet it is a world marked by ruthless cruelty where species preys on species and individual life-forms come into being to die and rot away. The world that men and women have created is far worse. The cruelty is no longer impersonal but willed and deliberate. It has taken on such local habitations and names as Auschwitz and Ravensbrück, as the Soviet labour camps whose names have not yet burned themselves into our western awareness, as the torture centres of the Argentine and Chile. In this kind of world the claims that Christianity makes can appear at once frivolous and blasphemous.

Yet if there were not some meaning to this wantonly inflicted suffering, if there were not some assurance that ultimately all shall be well and all manner of thing shall be well, life would risk appearing merely a cruel joke, the accidental by-product of some impassive cosmic process, and all our struggles and endeavours pointless. For me Christianity thus provides the assurance that what we do matters, that it is important whether we choose to do A rather than B. It provides the assurance that suffering will not go unrequited and unredressed, that the potential that is so often stunted or wasted will somehow come to fulfilment.

But is this simply the child's complaint: 'It isn't

fair'? Is living in a coldly impersonal, cruel, capricious and unjust universe simply a fact we have to accept, something it is no use whining about? There is no objective answer to this question. It is a matter of personal choice, of opting for what Hans Küng in *Does God Exist?* has called a fundamental trust in reality and in the God who sustains that reality. As far as I am concerned, the moral coherence offered by the God of Christianity rescues life from crumbling away into pointlessness and meaninglessness.

Nor is this God just some remote metaphysical principle. The core of Christian belief is that God became man. This extraordinary man Jesus gathered a group of disciples around him; and slowly they came to realise that in this man they had known and loved, in his life, his preaching, his death and resurrection, God was directly at work. Gradually this conviction crystallised out in the Chalcedonian formula that Jesus Christ is truly God and truly man. Keeping this in balance is something we find extraordinarily difficult. We are emerging from a period in which there has been so much emphasis on Jesus's divine nature as to obscure the fact that if the incarnation means anything it means that Jesus was a human being, not some heavenly visitant.

Being human means dying; and Jesus endured death in one of the crueller forms invented by perverse human ingenuity. Yet we believe that God raised him up to life in unimaginable fullness, and that we too are promised a share in this life. As far as I am concerned the 'how' of the resurrection is secondary: it is something we shall only find out when our turn comes to die. What matters is the 'that', the promise that our life is not doomed to the mocking denial of its purpose that death would seem to entail but will find its fulfilment in a way that we cannot imagine and cannot create for ourselves. The resurrection is thus crucial for me as the clinching assurance that life does have meaning.

In trying to work out why I personally am a Catholic I find that these have emerged as the primary considerations, and the question of belonging to the Catholic Church rather than any other Christian communion becomes a secondary one. This is strange, because becoming a Catholic was a deliberate choice when I was twenty. Moreover, the Church I joined was, as we have seen, very different from the Church of today. The early 1950s marked the last stage of that period of extreme triumphalism, juridicism and clericalism that disfigured the Church's history during the first half of this century. Yet the basic reasons that brought me into the Church are still, I think, valid despite all the learning and unlearning demanded by thirty years of rapid change.

There was, first of all, the element of authenticity, though this on its own would not necessarily have made me a Catholic as distinct from, say, an Anglican. It is very easy to hear in the gospel only what we want to hear, to see only what fits in with our particular biases and prejudices; and the more one is on the fringe of mainstream Christianity the easier it is to be led astray by these partial insights instead of being challenged by the gospel in its totality and by those disturbing sayings and stories that cut right across what we complacently take for granted. Hence the continual emphasis throughout the Church's history on going back to the source, on getting back to the pristine gospel without being led astray by all the later accretions that have grown up around it.

That in itself would seem to suggest the tradition of

the Reformation, which was after all aimed at purging the Church of all the corruptions that fifteen centuries of human waywardness had bred. But here the second element comes in: continuity and solidarity. If salvation means anything, then it must have been consistently mediated to men and women from the time that Jesus first preached the good news. We cannot turn round and un-Church whole periods of Christian endeavour when men and women were trying to shape their lives in keeping with this gospel, however quaint or even misguided some of their efforts may seem to us now. Nor can we rule out sections of the tradition by which that gospel has been transmitted to us, however corrupt and un-Christian they may have been. Nor, finally, can we claim that it is only at this or that point in our history that we enjoy the resources of scholarship and the historical perspective that enable us at last to see what the gospel is all about.

Being a Christian thus means for me somehow accepting and coming to terms with the whole of the Church's history and tradition, including all the disgraceful episodes that have marred the history of institutional Christianity – just as being human means learning to accept and come to terms with the whole of one's life, including all the episodes one wishes had never happened. We can never blot out our past, and if we try to do so, to pretend it never happened, the effect of building a falsehood into the foundations of our life is corrosively disastrous. All we can do is to try to come to terms with our past. Translated into the life of the Church, this does not mean trying to offer unconvincing excuses, as the old-style apologetics did, for such crimes as the massacre of Béziers, the practices of the Inquisition, the persecution of

Protestants, or the condemnation of Galileo. Rather, it means realising just how wrong they are and just how completely they contradict the gospel that is the Church's mandate, while recognising at the same time that the Church today is equally liable to betray its mission in ways that we may not be much bothered about but our descendants will come to regret. To use Hans Küng's language, the Church's 'un-nature' is inextricably bound up with its nature, and we cannot have one without the other. To my mind the specific temptation of Protestantism is trying to do just that, to create an angelic Church which is not the actual historical sinful Church of sinners.

Catholicism for me is thus something inclusive, not exclusive, comprehensive, not sectarian. And this is how the pull of Catholicism outweighs the loyalties that as an Englishman I cannot help feeling towards the Church of England. That Church claims to be the Church of the nation, but too often it comes over as the Church of that nation's ruling élite. It is no longer fair to deride it as the Tory party at prayer, but, particularly when it is observed in general synod assembled, it is only too tempting, if a little cruel, to see it as the English upper classes at prayer. By contrast the Catholic Church comes over as a Church of the people, and like Bernard Bergonzi I find this a great strength and comfort. Beyond this it has that element of universality which, despite the Anglican Communion being now world-wide and not even confined to the English-speaking world, the Church of England can never claim.

But the all-embracing aspect of Catholicism brings with it a temptation that is the counterpart of the Protestant one to separate out only those who measure up to a particular standard of righteousness. The Catholic temptation is to substitute human solidarity in sin for solidarity in redemption, to come to terms too easily with the ways of the world. Universality requires us to make the Christian message available to all men and women where they are so that it speaks to them in the language of their lives and circumstances and not in some foreign tongue that will pass them by. But all too easily this can slide into a dangerous complicity with the structures of human wickedness. Think of the priest on the quayside baptising newly captured Africans en masse before they were shipped across the Atlantic to work as slaves in Brazil.

There is a delicate tension that has to be maintained between welcoming men and women as they are and fulfilling the prophetic role that only the Church can fulfil. The Catholic temptation is to blur the prophetic witness for the sake of the welcome, to avoid disturbing the consciences of those acting in good faith. Yet there are signs here that the Church's leaders are becoming readier to speak out: witness the increasing outspokenness of US bishops on the question of nuclear weapons.

The third element involved in my becoming a Catholic was the need for certainty; and this, I suppose, is where my views have changed most. I had to learn that the kind of certainty I was hankering after is just not possible and would not be much use if it were. What I believe has to be what I believe, not my parrotting some formula gleaned from elsewhere. I can only reach this belief by the normal human process of learning, of trial and error. Of course there are moments of illumination when everything suddenly fits into place. Of course there is the need for guidance by those wiser than myself, and especially the accumulated wisdom of the past that is mediated to us by the Church's tradition. But there are no short cuts, no painless methods of learning without effort.

This applies, too, at the level of the Church as a whole. Like Louis McRedmond, I was lucky enough to find myself in Rome reporting the last two sessions of the Second Vatican Council, in my case for *The Tablet*. Like him, I had an almost palpable sense of the Holy Spirit being at work. But there was no question of this bishop or that theologian being struck by a shaft of divine revelation. Rather, the Holy Spirit was at work in and through the ordinary somewhat sordid human procedure of committees and haggling and behind-the-scenes intrigues. And, of course, what was needed was what was perhaps most remarkable about Vatican II: an assembly of the world's bishops willing to learn, open to new ideas, ready to listen.

Vatican II also marked a shift from extrinsic to intrinsic authority, from: 'Do this because I tell you to' to: 'Do this because it makes sense'. For me it meant that what had always been implicit in the Catholic faith now became explicit. I don't think I had ever taken something absolutely on trust, but on the understanding that, though I might not be able to see it at the time, it would eventually make sense and be seen to make sense. Vatican II speeded up this process and ensured that some reasonable justification had to be provided for every aspect of the Church's policy and teaching.

All this was latent when I became a Catholic, and no doubt if the Council had not taken place I would eventually have found the Church a very uncomfortable place to be. What helped me at the time, besides a patience and docility that have since worn a little thin, was the fact that some of the more disagreeable aspects of life in the Church, such as the denial of intellectual freedom, did not impinge directly on my life. And right from the start there were some aspects of what often passed for (and still passes for) Catholicism that I learned I could safely do without. The Dominican instructing me pointed out that, though we were bound to believe that hell existed, we were not bound to believe that any human souls had been consigned there. Unlike Bernard Bergonzi, I never took the Index very seriously: I was helped by being already at Oxford when I encountered Catholicism, and when a Catholic student who actually had a copy of the Index made a great point of keeping those books on it he possessed under lock and key, I took this as simply another undergraduate pose. I never developed a taste for miraculous medals and novenas and devotions like the nine first Fridays. Despite considerable effort, I found the rosary did not mean much for me as a form of prayer, and fairly soon I stopped being worried about this. Admittedly, I was and remain a somewhat lazy Catholic: Mass once a week is enough for me in the way of public worship.

The Council showed that the unpleasant and indefensible aspects of the Church's behaviour were not the price that had to be paid for being a Catholic, as up till then we were encouraged to think was the case. As Bishop Christopher Butler wrote just after the Council, in an admitted exaggeration, the Church before John XXIII 'was the best of all possible religions, and everything in it an intellectual scandal'. Now with the Council the Church could come out in favour of religious freedom not only without denying what it saw as its unique mission but as the only justifiable condition for that mission. Now the Mass did not have to be in a dead language which only a privileged few could understand and which too often was gabbled in a way that suggested the celebrant neither knew nor cared what he was saying.

The most dramatic change occurred over the Church's attitude to birth control. Indeed, what originally started me off on the long road towards becoming a Catholic was an argument on this topic with a fellow-undergraduate who happened to be a Catholic. To someone like myself, with a background of devout agnosticism laced with considerable exposure to the Bible and the Book of Common Prayer, it came as a shock to find apparently sane and rational people who could argue seriously that contraception was wrong. The argument from nature was an attractive one to a romantic soul like myself, and so too was the coherent Aristotelian style of argument that did not leave any awkward loose ends or unanswered questions.

At the time I got married even the idea of what has since become officially accepted as 'responsible parenthood' – in other words, birth control – was pretty well unheard of in the Catholic Church in England. One heard stories of parish priests calling on recently married women to enquire why they weren't pregnant. One's duty was to breed, and to drive the lesson home there were in the 1950s still Catholic bishops in England who made a point of officiating in person at the baptism of seventh and subsequent children. The safe period was known about, together with its concomitant paraphernalia of thermometers and temperature charts; but the accepted view of moral theologians, as it filtered down to the ordinary man and more particularly woman in the pew, was that this method could only be used for really serious reasons, and to ensure an adequate space between births rather than to limit their number. Large families were the ideal, and Catholics were urged to be generous.

What Catholics of our generation went through has been brilliantly described by David Lodge in his novels *The British Museum is Falling Down* and *How Far Can You Go?* When the question began to be publicly discussed within the Church it quickly became clear that, although the traditional condemnation of contraception had always been presented as a matter of natural law, which meant that in principle the reasons for it should appear convincing to anyone of good will, there were in fact no valid arguments to justify a total ban on 'artificial' methods of birth control in all circumstances. The distinction between natural and artificial came to seem increasingly tenuous and quite unable to support the absolute condemnation the traditional teaching required, while when you looked at it closely the argument from biology pointed the other way: sex in human beings is not confined to a period of oestrus or rut but seems designed (if talk of design is legitimate) at least as much to keep the couple together during the exceptionally long period needed to bring their offspring up as for begetting the offspring in the first place.

The mess the Church has got itself into over the question of birth control, with a teaching proclaimed by its official leadership (and not always with very much conviction, as is shown by the number of bishops who rushed for the nearest loophole when *Humanae vitae* came out in 1968) only to be repudiated in practice (and often in theory too) by the majority of its members, is a sad example of the retreat from the hopes the Council engendered. Our hopes may have been a little romantic and naïve; but, given what

Christianity is all about, were they that unrealistic? All we were looking for was a Church we would not continually have to be apologising for or, in some of its official stances, dissociating ourselves from.

The mess the Church is getting itself into over its treatment of the divorced and remarried is another sad example of this retreat. Marriage may be indissoluble in the sense of being meant to be for life; but there seems little point in using the concept of indissolubility to pretend that a marriage that has died and begun to fester is still alive when it so obviously is not, or to set up arbitrary obstacles to the peace of mind of those who have been through the trauma of a broken marriage. When annulments were few and far between, at least the Church's discipline had the merit of impartial cruelty; but now, when the canon lawyers have allowed a laudable compassion to prompt them into finding new reasons why a marriage that has broken down never was a marriage in the first place, it seems merely capricious and hypocritical. For the Catholic, coping with a dead marriage means being devious enough, or knowing a canon lawyer devious enough, to find the right loophole in what would otherwise be an impenetrable barrier to a second marriage recognised by the Church. And when the canon lawyers fail there are what are known as 'pastoral solutions': the readmission of divorced and remarried Catholics to the sacraments at the discretion of the priest concerned. I do not think there is any easy answer to this problem of coping with divorce and remarriage while at the same time trying to sustain the ideal of life-long marriage: witness the difficulties the Church of England has been experiencing in this field. But the problem will not go away merely by claiming that marriages ought not to break down or by treating divorce and remarriage as the one unforgivable sin.

Perhaps even sadder is the way the very modest proposals that emerged from the National Pastoral Congress held in Liverpool in 1980 have simply been stalled. The request for communion under both kinds to become the norm (as it already is in some parishes) met with sympathy from the English and Welsh bishops, as did the suggestion that general absolution (which, it has been found, leads to an increase and not a decrease in private confession) should be more generally used; but in both cases anything more than sympathy is blocked by Rome. In these circumstances suggestions for the ordination of married men to be considered, and even the possibility of women priests, have little if any hope of being taken up.

All this would seem to place me firmly among the members of His Holiness's loyal opposition. Yet I do not regard myself as a Catholic dissenter or as some kind of way-out radical. In fact the evidence of the National Pastoral Congress and of the survey of Catholic opinion conducted by Michael P. Hornsby-Smith and Raymond M. Lee of the University of Surrey suggests that my views and attitudes are typical of a considerable number of my fellow-Catholics, in some cases of the majority. But, particularly given the character of the present pope, we seem to have reached an impasse. Symptomatic is the way in which the bishops of England and Wales seem to have decided that it is no use at all trying to press Rome any further over the question of general absolution, which they see as fulfilling a genuine pastoral need by helping to bring about the formal reconciliation with the official Church of all those many Catholics who are put off by the whole business of confession (Mary Craig is not alone in keeping well clear of the confessional) but which Rome is trying to stop developing into a normal practice alongside the custom of individual private confession. If Rome is not prepared to accept the pastoral judgement of bishops on the spot on how the sacrament of penance can best be administered, what hope is there of it listening to the witness of married Catholics on birth control when this would involve admitting it had made a mistake?

But in a Church that has become as dangerously over-centralised as the Catholic Church has become, it is probably as well that its ordinary members should almost be forced to work out their own salvation for themselves instead of relying, as they had been encouraged to rely, on continual guidance from above. I have long thought it would have been disastrous if John XXIII had been succeeded by another pope with the same kind of prophetic vision. Instead, Paul VI tempered his continuation of John XXIII's revolution with the necessary reaction that was needed if that revolution was not going to be merely a superficial cosmetic change of fashion. James Mackey's image of birth is powerfully apposite. The only thing we need to remember is that, if labour is allowed to go on too long, you get an exhausted mother and risk the baby's injury or even death.

Yet it would be wrong to end on a carping note what has to serve as an introduction to the other essays on this theme as well as a personal account of why I believe what I believe. What we are all trying to do is to give an account of the hope that is in us, and however traumatic our experience of the Church has been we have found that it is to the Church that we owe this hope. Christianity is not something that can live in a vacuum. It is about the possibility of men and women actually learning to love and serve each other instead of exploiting each other. The Church's task is to make it possible for this to happen, and it is something that is perhaps more essential today than it has ever been: in a world armed with nuclear weapons, over-populated, and increasingly aware of the limited and fragile nature of its basic resources, Christianity in practice, with the qualities it demands of forbearance and unselfishness, has indeed become necessary for human survival. It is this essential task of reconciling us with God and with each other that is what matters.

Once a Catholic . . .

MARY CRAIG

2

Once a Catholic . . .

MARY CRAIG

IT WOULD BE HARD to imagine a more Catholic childhood than mine: I was eighteen before I even met anyone of another persuasion, or, as we so negatively put it, a non-Catholic. There were Catholics – and there was the rest of the human race who did not have that good fortune. Our town, St Helens in south Lancashire, was immensely proud of being the most Catholic town in England, a title hotly disputed by nearby Preston, but, so far as I know, never conceded. In St Helens you were never out of sight or sound of a Catholic church, each of them commanding the ferocious loyalty of its parishioners. One of my aunts who every Sunday walked half a mile to a church not her own – preferring its neo-Gothic architecture – was considered something of a traitor. Such defection was almost as reprehensible as attendance at 't' Parish Church', the town's Anglican church which stood in the main street opposite Woolworths and which we would have died rather than enter. No mosque, synagogue or pagoda could have seemed more alien.

My mother was a fervent daily Mass-goer, and, as my father had died just before I was born, she supported us both by teaching in a Catholic infants school. At the age of four, I was sent to the convent kindergarten which she herself had attended as a child, now ruled by a martinet called Sister Loretta. Here, among other things doubtless, we learned the penny catechism by heart, reciting the answers each day like well-drilled little parrots. We had spelling-bees and 'tables'-bees and most of all catechism-bees, and woe betide us if we didn't know the answers. Every so often a visiting priest would come and examine us, an experience we both dreaded and enjoyed. Probably the enjoyment was more in evidence, since we showed off and were rewarded by sweets and a half-holiday from school.

Religion was in the air we breathed, whether at school or at home. Our nuns belonged to an order founded by Mère Julie Billart, who has now been canonised. Mère Julie loomed large in our lives. We used to perform plays in which she figured as heroine, and I remember an exciting scene in which she was being smuggled across Belgium in a hay-cart which the militia were prodding with bayonets (I don't remember why or when). In the last scene she was a nun on her deathbed and we all sang her favourite hymn, 'The good God is so very good'.

Each of us had our guardian angel, to whom, we were constantly assured, we were a grave disappointment, so steeped were we in sin. Various punishments were tried (we were never beaten or caned) to no avail. One of these was at least original though hardly calculated to inspire us with a love for religion – we were sent to the chapel to repent. The chapel was on the other side of the convent, along corridors and up two flights of stairs. Because of its isolation it was an eerie place. One friend was sent there and then forgotten until the nuns assembled for compline at six – by which time her mother was nearly frantic.

It was so much easier to sin than not to sin, and I decided at an early age that the only safe course would be to remain locked in a room doing nothing at all. But then one would have been guilty of sins of omission – not doing what one ought was just as bad as doing what one ought not. We hadn't heard of Catch 22, but we were caught in it. I had one particularly grievous 'sin' which I found it hard to kick: I used to secrete Monday's penny for black babies and spend it on aniseed balls which were twenty for a penny at Mr Dennett's cavernous sweet-shop opposite the school. Once I bought thirty, and my greed was my undoing. When my crime was discovered, there was Hell to pay. I could never be sure whether this sin was 'mortal' or not. If it was 'venial' it didn't matter so much, but 'mortal' left a mark on your soul that couldn't be washed off. I worried about this, not knowing how you could ever tell. My nightmares were alternately of myself as some spectral Lady Macbeth forever unable to wash away the stain of my sins, or (less often because less likely) of the petrifying boredom of an unending harp session in Heaven. I didn't much care for the idea of eternity.

Just before I was six, we began our training for first confession and first holy communion. Confession came first. I remember the day quite clearly because I had a terrible sin to come to terms with. A girl of fourteen looked after me at home, and one day, in a fit of petulance, I had smacked her on the place where she sat down. She was outraged, my mother was outraged, there was a general *air de crise*. I was duly penitent, and scared to death because my first confession was looming. How could I possibly describe my crime? The portion of anatomy I had whacked was unmentionable, and alas I could not bring myself to name it. The parish priest, Father Riley, a lovable and eccentric old man who kept a pet alligator in his baptismal pool, suspected I was holding out on him, but he could not prise the horrid truth from me. 'I smacked her ... face,' I finally blurted out, thus telling a lie in my first confession and convincing myself that I was thereby doomed for all time.

It was with no little trepidation therefore that I approached my first communion. Had I not already joined the ranks of the damned? Sister Loretta did not help matters by telling us a story of a naughty little girl called Alice who, though told to keep her head bowed after she had received the sacred wafer, had a peep at her mother and father going up to the communion rail. She died of remorse or something soon after. This would surely be my fate. I waited in terror for the great day, and the fact that my head almost touched my knees until Mass was safely over owed more to my fear of imminent death than to any innate piety. Oh Alice, Alice, how you haunted my childhood!

In fact my first approach to all the sacraments of the Church seemed doomed, and my guardian angel must have had a lot of explaining to do. On the day I was to be confirmed I accidentally swallowed some toothpaste water in the morning, and, in spite of this infraction of the abstinence laws, hadn't the nerve to tell my mother I should not be able to receive communion. So I was 'not in a state of grace' when I went up to the communion rail, and to this day I can recall the anguish of being confirmed by the bishop that afternoon, in the sure conviction that Hell had opened wide its gates for me.

Every morning I was despatched to the eight

o'clock Mass at the Jesuit church which lay on the short route between home and school. When I skipped this chore, someone always told my mother. On Sundays, of course (and throughout Lent, and on all holy days), only death could have provided an adequate excuse for not going to Mass. And not only Mass. At three or thereabouts my mother and I set off for Benediction. It was generally understood that, though you had already done your bit by going to Mass, throwing in Benediction as well placed salvation beyond reasonable doubt. It was a gilt-edged insurance policy, as were little extras like indulgences (so many days off Purgatory if you said a certain prayer or went to Mass on certain days), Mass on First Fridays of the month and as many Masses as possible on All Souls' Day. One woman in our parish was reverently said to have notched up nine, though I could never work out how she had managed it.

Twice a month on a Saturday I went to confession, joining the long queues of penitents waiting outside the half dozen confessionals. The trick was to choose the priest who kept you the shortest time and gave the lightest penance. Outside the boxes of the more censorious there were no penitents at all. When it was my turn, I rushed through the whole business as though a train was after me: 'Bless-me,-Father-for-I-have-sinned,-it-is-two-weeks-since-my-last-confession,-I-have-been-disobedient-told-lies-and-told-tales.' Only then did I draw breath. Where I got that pathetic little trilogy from I have no idea, but I trotted it out every fortnight. The poor confessor must have died of boredom if everyone else was like me. Regularly he gave me three 'Hail Mary's' and I would then hurtle through the act of contrition, terrified of forgetting it in the middle. I did often wonder about contrition. I could imagine what we were told was the 'imperfect' variety – feeling sorry for one's sins because they might send you to the flames of Hell. But 'perfect' contrition – disinterested sorrow because one had offended God – made no sense to me; I tried to imagine it but could not. Maybe it was only for the saints. If God had any reality for me, it was as an all-powerful tyrant waiting for me to trip myself up. How could I be expected to love such a sacred monster?

Sometimes I was so bored by my mindless little list of sins that I longed to have something more exciting to confess – like murder; but as I grew older I discovered I had no mechanism for coping with guilt. It weighed me down. After my first kiss I went into the confessional as though to the guillotine: 'Father, is it wrong to be kissed?' I ventured to ask. 'It all depends...' began my aged confessor, and I emerged about ten minutes later, thoroughly confused, aware only that he had explained to me that I could legitimately kiss my grandfather. This seemed both curious and undesirable and it didn't do much for my conscience either. I felt no wiser, only guiltier.

Two of my father's sisters were nuns and they could not have been more different from each other. One was a strict novice mistress in the Notre Dame order, the other an easy-going Sister of Charity, one of those who wore the big winged bonnets. I was somewhat scared of my novice-mistress aunt who expected me always to be on my best behaviour, remember to bow to Sister Superior when she came into the room, and cross my ts properly when I wrote letters. I adored the other one, Gretta (who was also in awe of her elder sister), a tireless worker among the down-and-outs in the East End of London, full of loving kindness and human warmth. She let little girls be little girls and didn't object to muddy feet and large appetites. At Notre Dame we were proffered dainty cucumber sandwiches on a tray (my father was reputed to have once piled them all on top of each other, eaten them in one and said: 'Now, when do we eat?'), but Aunt Gretta's tiny convent smelt of baking, and while I ate plates of thick ham and slabs of fruit cake, this large motherly woman would bustle round encouraging me to have more. I dare say she hadn't heard of calories. I think my Aunt Gretta was the first really holy and completely human person I ever met and I recall her with real gratitude.

All through the lower school we went on with the penny catechism, although I don't think the more interesting commandments were dealt with at any length. We had a little purple book of 'Bible Narratives' too, which was all we learned of the Old Testament. (I was always under the impression that the Bible, i.e. the Old Testament, was a Protestant book.) I have a vision of myself in the Upper Third frantically committing to memory large slices of St Mark's gospel, so as to be the first to rush out and be 'heard' by the teacher. My memory being what it was (wonderful only in the short term) I'd probably forgotten it all by the following week. In any case I didn't find it any more compelling than the poems we had to learn. If anything, 'The Lady of Shalott', 'The Listeners' and 'The Forsaken Merman' had more resonance and stayed longer in the mind.

Outside our school, the Lowe House church carillon played a verse of *Salve Regina* every hour, and single lines on the quarter. Our Lady of course was important in our lives, and when we transgressed we were said to have offended her. Perhaps because I was brought up at home by one mother, two aunts and one nursemaid, with no siblings and not a male in sight (to say nothing of the nuns at school), I felt no enthusiasm for yet another female authority figure, though I dared not give voice to such a disgraceful point of view. Mary was our model; we put flowers in front of her statue, and each year in May we had our own special day on which to wear a miraculous medal on a large blue ribbon round our necks. The glory of that day was rivalled only by the Corpus Christi procession in June. Wearing white, with veils held in place by artificial snowdrops, we sang Latin hymns and processed round the church grounds in brilliant sunshine. (Beforehand we besieged Our Lady with prayers for good weather, and, so far as I remember, it was always fine.)

In the processions we looked and felt like little angels, but in the classroom the nuns appraised us more realistically. The old nun who took us for school certificate religion read our exam papers and assured us that our only hope of passing lay in beseeching our guardian angels to change the papers. As I was awarded a distinction mark, mine must have come up trumps. This same nun told us more than once that we should not use the word 'body' or think at all about our bodies. For modesty's sake we were supposed to avert our eyes while bathing. This went deep and I was already a half-way Manichee when one day our head-mistress summoned the Fifth Form. We had been invited to a dance that evening run by the local Christian Brothers' Catholic grammar school. The head expressed her horror at the discovery that so many of us were going. Good Catholic girls like ourselves, she shuddered, had no business attending events where we were likely to be (and I quote) 'pawed by boys'. Docile though we were, her comments shocked us deeply. Another of her colleagues had earlier told us that if we were asked to dance by a young man, we must first inquire whether he was a Catholic.

Towards the end of my schooldays, three incidents stand out. The first certainly traumatised me; I'm less sure about the other two. A Jesuit father who gave our sixth form Easter retreat told us that he found it extremely distasteful to place the communion wafer on a girl's tongue. Inhibited as I already was, the effect of this discourse was to frighten me off receiving the sacrament for over thirty years. Only when communion in the hand became allowable (and by that time I was past forty-five) did I muster the courage to approach the communion rail except where circumstances made it unavoidable. Quite recently, during a lecture tour of Malta (where communion in the hand is frowned on), I experienced the old sick panic at the thought of receiving the wafer on the tongue and I knew that I was physically incapable of it.

The second incident was ludicrous. It occurred during a particularly boring religious knowledge session, based on the 'apologetics' approach which was then in favour (Catholics could have all the answers provided they took the trouble to learn them). Bored beyond my limits, I scribbled on a piece of paper the name of a boy from our church and flicked it across to my neighbour. She retaliated in kind. Whereupon Sister D pounced. Consternation, shock, horror, wringing of hands, cries of mortal sin. (What was it? Incipient sexual perversion?) My neighbour and I, left to pace the corridor for two hours while our fate was decided, were finally and solemnly banned from joining the Children of Mary. A terrible fate. Six months later the decree was rescinded and we were allowed to join, but to underline my own greater wickedness, I was given a medal of inferior quality (tin!).

Incident number three was probably the sequel to that. Most of the Sixth Form belonged to the Young Christian Students, a group which each year performed Hilary Pepler's mime of the Passion during Holy Week. Being tall, dark and reasonably good at acting, I was chosen to play the part of Jesus. Fate, in the guise of our headmistress, decreed otherwise. Arriving for the first rehearsal, I found her waiting for me. 'You,' she cried accusingly, 'are not to play Jesus. I have a more suitable part in mind.' She had. I played Mary Magdalen, a prestigious role but intended in this instance as a monumental put-down. (Here I should perhaps put on record that my reputation with the nuns was quite unjustified. My innocence was such that not until some years later did I actually learn about the facts of life. The significance of the choice of Mary Magdalen didn't dawn on me till then.)

Such was my schooling in religion in the forties. Mary O'Malley's play, *Once A Catholic*, was gruesomely real for me and my contemporaries. ('It *couldn't* have been like that,' protested the friend who saw it with me. 'No, in some respects it was worse,' I agreed.) I left the convent at seventeen with inhibitions impenetrable, a deep fear of life, an armoury of draconian laws to govern my every action and no sense at all of a loving God. It was only because I dared not do otherwise that I continued to call myself Catholic.

In all fairness, it was not the nuns' fault. They were

prisoners of a narrow outmoded view of religion, and some of them knew it. When change eventually came, nuns throughout the country welcomed it, putting the past behind them, revising their constitutions with intelligence and enthusiasm. They, like the rest of us, were in need of fresh air.

But when I left school the wind of change was not yet blowing. Vatican II was not even a twinkle in anyone's eye, and the Church was at its last gasp of triumphalism and legalism. That, I thought, was the way it had always been and would always be – I could not conceive of change. Perhaps already on the continent of Europe – now emerging from a catastrophic war – there were rumblings and mutterings of change, but no suspicion of them had reached Catholic Lancashire.

Would I have stayed a Catholic if things had not changed? I like to think that I would not, because my reasons would have been the wrong ones. In the years that elapsed between school and the Council I stayed put in a half-hearted way, though one by one many of my friends 'lost their faith'. Contraception was the usual reason, but the cause of their defection went deeper than that, since one or two of them became violently anti-Catholic. 'Why do you stay?' they asked me, knowing how lukewarm I was. Why indeed? I had no real answers, only one on a par with Pascal's wager. Better be safe than sorry, better to hedge one's bets. My religion was a formula and it bored me, but I saw it as insurance. I didn't admit to myself that my 'faith' was non-existent. I attended Sunday Mass and avoided (I hoped) mortal sin for fear of a possible unimaginable Hell. Was that faith?

At Oxford I joined the chaplaincy and it became the focal point of my social life. Indeed I met my husband there. Frank, like myself, was a cradle Catholic, his own religious upbringing not very different from my own, though boys, I think, were less vulnerable than girls, more likely to emerge unscathed. We were both law-abiding Catholics, which meant that when we married in the early fifties we accepted the Church's ban on artificial birth control and trusted hopefully to the 'safe period'. It spelled death to spontaneity and romance, and a lot of Catholic marriages foundered on the rock of so much constraint. Even the safe period had to be used with moderation, since the primary aim of a true Catholic marriage was procreation and this aim could not be set aside for purely selfish reasons. David Lodge has said it all in his wickedly funny novel, *How Far Can You Go?* That was our period: its problems, hilarious to the outsider, were real and devastating.

We had four children, all boys. Two of them were mentally handicapped, and the first of these, Paul, could not hear or speak or even recognise us. He was a full-time charge on my time and there seemed to be no compensation for such misery. Yet this was the watershed in my life, the period when I simultaneously came unstuck and found a kind of faith.

If I refused to let self-pity take a hold, it was only because I knew it would destroy me. It was self-preservation, not spiritual wisdom. But self-pity was always lurking, and as time went on and matters got worse as I got more exhausted, my resistance to it weakened. I remember at my lowest point reading an article in my eldest child's encyclopaedia: about the cosmos, the galaxies, the endless unknown spaces. In despair I repudiated at last the God of my childhood, not understanding He was no more than an idol anyway. Man was a tiny dot adrift in space, he was not the centre of the universe as I had believed. I was gripped by a sense of the absurdity of everything, and I said goodbye to what had passed for faith in my life.

I had touched bottom. Shortly after this I went to cook and make beds for a week at the Sue Ryder Home in Cavendish, Suffolk – to escape my own problems by taking refuge in someone else's. That week changed my life. At Cavendish for the first time I met real suffering, and I saw the courage and quiet dignity with which it was confronted. Some of those whom I met that week had been to hell and back – the Hell of such places as Auschwitz, Majdanek and Buchenwald. The shock of discovering what life had done to them forced me to look at my own life in a clearer perspective. I had a strange persistent feeling that I had been brought to this place to discover something of value. At Cavendish that week, seeing men and women whose lives had been stripped of everything that had seemed to give them meaning, I glimpsed the truth that the real needs of a human being are much simpler than we imagine, and that it often takes great suffering to reveal that to us. And if in the midst of our own distress we stretch out a hand to help someone else, the gesture unlocks something within us and enables us to discover a little of our own hidden, even unsuspected resources.

When I returned home, it was as though I had come alive again. I didn't use the word 'God' (it's a word I am still uncomfortable with) – but at Cavendish I had found that people's lives held a deep core of meaning, and that the meaning was there for me too. Slowly I came to face my own situation with Paul, trying to see it exactly as it was, neither playing it down nor exaggerating.

And then Nicky was born, nine years after Paul –

another handicapped child, this time a mongol. It was too much. The precarious edifice of acceptance reeled and tottered. But amazingly it did not collapse. The night after Nicky's birth, when I was punch-drunk with hopelessness, I had the sudden overwhelming conviction of being held firm, the inexplicable sense of 'all shall be well and all shall be well and all manner of thing shall be well', which Julian of Norwich expressed so poignantly. I was no mystic and the experience remains unique in my life. But while it lasted I had an almost tangible awareness of someone or something working within and beyond me, helping me to see a deeper reality behind the apparent disaster. Call it what you will. As I write this I have just heard a woman describe an almost identical experience on the radio, ascribing it tentatively to 'mother Nature'. What's in a word? It is the momentary sense of all things working together for good, of a fundamental unity at the heart of creation, that is important.

At times of acute depression I have often again doubted that the world or ourselves have any meaning. But I cannot really conceive of a world that is a spiritual vacuum. If I say that since that time I have been a 'religious person', I am making no claims for my behaviour (which is no better and possibly worse than other people's); I am stating my belief that beyond what I am and beyond the created world there is a great unexplained mystery; that in some way related to this mystery I am responsible for my life and what I do with it; that I have my share of responsibility for the world; and that I am on a journey whose course is uncharted but which will take me nearer to the heart of the mystery. As a friend of mine, Monica Furlong, once wrote: 'The journey is not to "catch" God, even though it moves in the direction that men have called God. It is to become what is in one to become.' Whether one uses a small or large 'r', whether one uses the word 'God' or not, that is essentially the religious quest, and it is inescapably mine until I die, however badly I may fail to measure up to it.

So the birth of my mongol son marked not an end but another beginning. For the first time I began to perceive life as a gift which had to be used. I began to see that my own 'bad' experience was not all bad; through the insights I had gained from it, I could perhaps help other people make sense of their lives. If it was possible I wanted to deepen these insights by reading.

It was Harry Williams's book *The True Wilderness* which shed the first light on those dead mental constructs of my Catholic childhood. These sermons preached to (Anglican) students in Cambridge were a revelation to me. Suddenly I was reading words about sin, repentance, redemption, atonement which actually made sense and had a relevance to my life, here, now. I was riveted. Possibly these insights were not new, but they were certainly new to me. Poised between the twin terrors of isolation and absorption, Williams seemed to say, the human being needed more light rather than more strength, a growth in inner understanding. The destructive forces which threaten us (and to avoid which we seek every kind of distraction) were what overwhelmed Jesus of Nazareth in the garden of Gethsemane. Reading *The True Wilderness*, the inaccessible Man/God of my convent school became flesh and blood, and his agony became real. As a child I had tried and failed to be moved by that scene in the garden, but now, when

I could imagine it as compounded of dread, sense of failure and an agonisingly clear vision of man's blindness and stupidity, pity flooded in.

Never before had anyone made me see 'redemption' as 'becoming a full human being', and that was the biggest revelation of all. So that was what Jesus had done – not so much founded the Roman Catholic Church as shown what it meant to be a truly integrated human being. Jesus, the representative man, trusting completely in the truth which he had been charged to pass on, showed what each of us could become through the power of unselfregarding love. His great task was that of reconciling men to themselves, to each other and to God.

I can't say that I experienced instant conversion, but I felt the marvellous relief of things falling into place. 'Redemption' was no longer an empty word, but something in which I had to share. It wasn't a question of achieving perfection (something none of us can achieve, given all the obstacles in our way) but of being extended as far as one's own unique possibilities allow, and of helping others to do the same. 'Thou shalt love thy neighbour *as thyself.*'

In my catalogue of rediscovery, the Catholic Church came last and fairly late. The Second Vatican Council had not affected me very much. I had loved Pope John, and had been sad when he died. Of course I knew he had summoned an Ecumenical Council, and had vaguely wondered what 'ecumenical' meant – without bestirring myself to find out. The Council was long over when I discovered it, mainly through a Jesuit priest with whom I became friendly, and the mother of a pupil of mine who was a fan of Hans Küng's. Exasperated by my indifference she presented me with a copy of *The Council and Reunion* for

Christmas one year. About a year later I got round to reading it, and when I started I couldn't stop. I went on to read everything that Küng had written. I didn't know then that Küng was regarded as the devil incarnate by traditionalist Catholics – what concerned me was that a Church community such as he described made sense. The emergence of a Church which no longer saw itself in militant terms as an impregnable fortress, but as a group of people on a pilgrimage towards God, all too capable of mistakes but capable also of learning from them – the emergence of such a Church was exhilarating.

Fifteen years have passed since then and I have come closer to being a full-fledged Catholic. Not completely fledged, however, since I have not been near a confessional box in those years, and to many Catholics that will put me beyond the pale. I am still diffident about acknowledging the label 'Catholic', but then I am still diffident about the shorthand word 'God' – which in no way detracts from my belief in what Bishop Butler prefers to call 'The Absolute Mystery'. I find the word 'God' makes something real and living into a lifeless idol: to fix and name something essentially unfixable and un-nameable seems to me to run the risk of idolatry, of making 'God' in our own image. I cannot answer a straight 'Yes' when I'm asked if I believe in God, because I'm not at all sure that the questioner and I mean the same thing. I have indeed known many self-styled unbelievers who are more on my wavelength on this matter than are some believers. Acknowledging oneself to be C of E, RC or anything else does not necessarily make one a believer. My belief in a unity which underlies all created things and in a reality which is deeper than anything we can yet know remains unshakeable. I believe too that this reality is the fountainhead of all that is valuable and good in our experience – the truth, beauty, wisdom and love that constantly remind us that we are capable of being better than we are; the peace and harmony that we occasionally glimpse even in the midst of the discord and strife which we have inherited and to which we add our share. And as this reality is the source of everything that goes to the making of person-ality, I believe that it is, in a way that I cannot comprehend, personal, the essence of personhood.

As a Christian I believe that Jesus of Nazareth was a complete revelation of this 'personhood', a clue to human nature as it is capable of becoming. In him we see human-ness defined and made authentic. He gave the world an entirely new understanding of God and of God's relationship to man. And he pointed to the human task of restoring unity, peace, harmony and love to the world, claiming to be 'the light of the world' and 'the way, the truth, and the life'. The best possible guide, it seems to me, for life's dark and difficult journey.

And if the resurrection is often a stumbling-block to belief in Jesus himself, perhaps it's because too much of the discussion has centred on 'the empty tomb', which may not be the crux of the matter. The essential thing is that something happened to change the timid disciples – who had run away at the first hint of trouble and had gone into hiding after the crucifixion 'for fear of the Jews' – into a group of people who were full of joy and confidence, ready to accept rejection and death for the sake of spreading the good news. The 'something' was their certainty that they had seen, heard, touched Jesus, after his death, that this man was the Christ – the word or sign or revelation from God to man. Once we can believe, as they did, that Jesus of Nazareth lives on as the risen Christ, we can accept that in him we can touch God, as in no other being who has ever lived, however holy. We experience resurrection in our own lives, when the pain of loss or failure gives rise to a new wisdom and a sense of being more deeply alive. In my own life it had been the recognition that in the midst of suffering we can be brought to understand that what reconciles and heals is ultimately stronger than what divides and destroys. It's a SEEING that doesn't just console me (though it does). It demands a total commitment from me. And isn't that the message of the Christ? Holiness, 'costing not less than everything', as Eliot said.

I have met other Christs along the way, people who have illuminated some part of life's truth for me. People like Mother Teresa or Dom Helder Camara say more about divine love than a thousand sermons could. Holy, whole, healed: the affinity between the words becomes apparent in people like them. God speaks to us through people, making us aware sometimes of an extra dimension. I remember my first meeting with Dom Helder and how, at a crowded reception, this tiny, wizened, nut-brown little man seemed to fill the entire room. I've had the same feeling on other occasions, with people whose human warmth reaches out to me, making me feel accepted, loved – and forgiven. There was an old nun I once knew in Belgium, crippled and in constant pain, yet shedding serenity around her. She taught me that holiness has little to do with the rule book and everything to do with an open heart. I owe to her the understanding that, whatever my failures and transgressions, forgiveness and mercy would always be at hand, enabling me to pick myself up and start again. Later on I found the same profoundly liberating conviction of God's limitless mercy in Julian of Norwich, but it was Mère Lioba who first offered me that priceless understanding. She shed light on the 'perfect contrition' that had eluded me as a child. In the face of such mercy, I could indeed feel the sorrow for my failure, that had nothing to do with fear of retribution.

By now I was a Christian by conviction, but was I a Catholic? From about 1970 I worked as the token Catholic on an ecumenical team on BBC radio (though I refused to handle such obviously 'Catholic' items as processions or apparitions of the Virgin Mary), I was a member of the bishops' mass media commission and I worked with the Jesuits at Farm Street, on their literary magazine *The Month*. I also soon became TV critic for the *Catholic Herald*. But I made no pretence of being an orthodox Catholic, describing myself always as being on the fringes of the Church. The description may well still fit, but I have finally opted for the Church in which I was born and baptised, because I need a spiritual home and because, if I want to call myself a Christian, a private, personal religion is a contradiction in terms. I must be a member of a living community.

There's a lot to be said for staying within the bounds of the known and familiar, within the ambiance which one knows and the idiom which one can understand. Even if some would deny me the appellation, I could never really be other than Catholic. Here I stand, I can no other. I am Catholic in the way that I am English and that I am a woman – it's part of what I am, affecting the way I see the world. It's the way I have been inserted into life. I was born at a time when the Catholic Church was at its most triumphalist and authoritarian worst, and the nuns who taught me had been born into that same supremely self-confident world. They were themselves the victims of blinkered teaching and over-rigorous dogmatism, and they were simply passing it on to us. Their lives were narrow and restricted and they confined us within the same negative prohibitions as bound them. It took the Vatican Council to liberate them. Today's nun is very different.

In any case there was always a good side. At least I was taught that what I did mattered. ('God looks after his own, Mary,' my headmistress used to sigh, as once again I appeared before her on some charge. How I wished that he would look after someone else for a change! Everyone mattered. Black babies mattered. Laugh if you will at the idea that our pennies would save a black baby for Jesus. That kind of missionary idea has been discredited, but it did teach us that there were people in the world for whom we were responsible. We were never taught to put our own cravings and impulses first, and we always knew that other people were to be valued for what they were rather than for what they had. Those years did not bring me faith, but they may have sowed a seed. In this context, it's worth recalling a story told me by an old friend from those days. She had taken her daughter – the product of a vast, famous, impersonal and highly secular London comprehensive – to see *Once A Catholic* at Wyndham's Theatre. 'Was it really like that?' the daughter asked. My friend, expecting outraged sympathy, said that indeed it was. 'Then you don't know how lucky you were,' said the girl.

But I must now make a more positive statement of my position. I believe that Christianity is the truest of all the revelations of God's message to man. I find great riches in Judaism, Buddhism, Hinduism and Islam, but they do not offer the completeness of the Christian message. As a Christian I must commit myself to a community. And when I look at the various Christian Churches, I see the Roman Catholic Church as the group that has struggled and straggled through history with the message of reconciliation and forgiveness intact: fallible, peccable, often and blatantly wrong, but still in business. Its behaviour at times in its history has been appalling, and nothing is gained by denying that. I squirm when I think of the religious intolerance, the persecutions, intrigues, inquisitions, politickings, *suppressiones veri*, resistance to new discoveries, and obfuscation of old ones; the injustices done to groups and individuals; the isolationism, triumphalism, authoritarianism, juridicalism and all the other isms which have bedevilled it. The list is endless, the case proven. But we shouldn't really be surprised that an institution made up of errant human beings should stand convicted of error, even gross error. Original sin does not exempt Churchmen from its grip. As an insider, I am forced to admit that unsavoury things are still going on. (Let me declare myself, and say I dislike the measures taken against Küng and threatened against Schillebeeckx and the present attempt to bring the Jesuits into line.)

But the Church is more than the sum of its imperfections, and all human nature without exception is flawed. There must be a necessary distinction between the Church as she is and the Church as she ought to be and would like to be. And alongside the awfulness don't let's forget the good. In a sense there are two histories of the Church – one of a marvellous clear vision and self-denying love, the other of an intolerant pettiness of spirit: Dr Jekyll and Mr Hyde in one body. Such a long record of painful searching after truth, of loving care, of forgiveness, of tenderness and healing is as difficult to explain – and raises at least as many questions – as the darker side of the Church's progress through history. In one sense, the fact that it is travel-stained and a little shoddy is the outward sign of its antiquity, of its unceasing pilgrimage through time. And the fact that it has survived scandals and corruptions which in any other organisation would have destroyed all credibility, at least hints that there is a power at work in it which may be, as it claims, divine.

No other Christian body actually claims to be the one, true, holy and apostolic Church, the heir to that original infant *ecclesia* which set out to proclaim the good news to all ages and cultures. I believe that the Spirit of God has remained with that community in spite of all its imperfections, and that its accumulated wisdom is worthy of a hearing. I don't believe that scripture had the last word to say. The lived Christian experience has surely had an importance too.

As it is actually met today in its official representatives, its churches and schools in all their variety, its clubs, societies and prayer groups, the Roman Catholic Church is clearly trying to make people more alive, more sensitive, more willing to listen to others, to attempt to heal all who are leading a damaged existence. Of course the intention is often greater than the achievement, a lot of its initiatives are misguided, a lot of the people who work in it and for it are odd or bigoted or intolerant or ineffectual. But at least they have good ends in mind. And when we think about it, it is startling to realise how much of the dreariest, least rewarding and most self-forgetful work that has to be done in any society is done by people linked to the Church and basically because of their Christian Faith. (This, of course, is true of all the Christian denominations.)

The sermons preached at Sunday Mass are often boring and full of bad theology or empty piety (*pace* my parish priest who is not guilty of any of these things) but taken altogether something unmistakable comes through: a positive message of hope and trust and love, the assurance of human dignity, the confidence that we are capable of choosing to be better than we are. The contrast between this and the messages we receive from the other areas of life is quite striking: spoil yourself, get in first, get them before they get you, buy-now-pay-later, you are what you own, nothing succeeds like success, and acceptance as a person hinges on the deodorant or hair spray you use, or on whether you've clawed your way to possession of an American Express card. 'Money, money, money, always sunny, in the rich man's world' – as the Abba song assures us. No wonder people are in despair: they ask for bread and are given froth.

By temperament I'm a loner and non-joiner, more at home in my study than in a crowd. But in the Church I have my community. I have the sense of an invisible network of people reacting on each other even at opposite poles of the world. Being a Catholic includes a strange consciousness of ideas, insights and traditional wisdom somehow seeping into one, and of a power being made available through the prayer of other members of this unseen network. Sometimes the invisible community becomes visible: when travelling, it's often reassuring to discover that a complete stranger is a fellow-Catholic. Though he (or she) may be of a different race or culture, it is an immediate bond. It's an experience which makes the idea of the Church's universality very real.

Anything less than this would seem to me too narrow, and narrow is the exact opposite of catholic, a word which implies touching everything in life. It is ironic and sad that to many outsiders it is the narrowness of the Catholic Church which is repellent. They are right to be repelled. The Church is only being Catholic when it enlarges our vision of the created world, of man and his relationship with his fellow-man and with God. I regret that the Church still presents itself in such negative terms: I am as dismayed as anyone by abortion, but it sometimes seems to be the only issue about which the Church is concerned. Ethics are only part of what the Church is about, a necessary underpinning, it's true, but I wish I heard more about healing, about forgiveness, about reconciliation.

Yet I do hear those things. I hear them from Pope John Paul. The Pope's conservatism often seems very negative. But if he seems too often to be inveighing *against* something, he is more often triumphantly *for* something – man. (And I am not sufficiently feminist to object to the word. No other will do as well.) 'How is a human being to be measured?' he asked the young people in Warsaw. 'By his physical strength? his senses? his intellectual powers? No – I tell you that man can only be measured in terms of the heart.' Over and over he speaks of the innate dignity and absolute worth of every human being – and he points to Christ as the key. Only through Christ, the redeemer of man, can man understand himself and the heights of which he is capable.

Amen, amen to that. I rest my case there.

Upon this Rock

PIERS PAUL READ

3

Upon this Rock

PIERS PAUL READ

IN TWENTY YEARS of adult life I have never for a moment doubted either the teachings or the disciplines of the Catholic Church.

The historical reasons for my Catholicism are these. In 1933 my mother, Margaret Ludwig, then a professional musician and lecturer in music at Edinburgh University, was converted to the Roman Catholic faith. Some months after she had been received into the Church she fell in love with my father, Herbert Read, who was professor of fine art at the same University. He was married with a ten-year-old son.

They ran off to London, and after my father's divorce were married in a registry office. My mother bore four children of whom I was the third. Her respect for my father's intelligence was reverential – she had German blood in her veins – but never for a moment was she inclined to adopt his agnosticism. Her faith was stronger than his reason, and almost as if to propitiate the God whom she had offended by her adulterous liaison, she brought us all up in the religion which denied her its sacraments and condemned her to Hell-fire.

I myself was baptised at the church of St Teresa in Beaconsfield when exactly nine months old. I was taught the rudiments of religion by my mother, and at the age of eight was sent to be educated by Benedictine monks. Faith preceded reason in my mind and has preserved its precedence ever since.

This faith developed not because of my upbringing but despite it. I disliked Gilling and Ampleforth, where I went to school, for what still seem to be quite proper reasons. Family life should be the basis of a Christian upbringing, and boarding schools undermine it. Moreover the public school values which the monks were so eager to instill into their pupils were less Christian than pagan Greek. There were among the monks both good and intelligent men, but they were all tainted by that pervasive snobbery which is so frequently found among English Catholics. At fifteen I schemed to leave Ampleforth, and might have left the Church as well had it not been for a secular priest, Michael Hollings, who came to Ampleforth to give a retreat and told me to distinguish between the school and the religion.

I also rebelled in adolescence against most of the values of my fervent, strong-willed mother and should by rights have gone over to the agnostic humanism of my father, whom I not only loved but admired. 'How can anyone,' he wrote, 'with a knowledge of the comparative history of religions retain an exclusive belief in the tenets of any particular sect?' He had that knowledge, and gently mocked the monks I had come to despise, but never for a moment was I tempted to adopt his scepticism and abandon my Catholic beliefs. The very remoteness and serenity of his paternal love made it easier to conceive of God the Father.

Even at sixteen, when I left school, my faith was neither naïve nor blind. It had given me such a taste for philosophical enquiry that when I went up to Cambridge I applied to read moral sciences rather than history to refine and deepen my beliefs.

The faculty of moral sciences at the end of the 1950s was in the hands of the most austere and pedantic of linguistic philosophers. They were agnostic not just about the existence of God but about the existence of the table upon which they laid their notes. For some months I persevered in the course of studies they offered, hoping that we might progress from the proofs of the table's existence to something more substantial. We did not. I suspected, though without the confidence to be sure, that the attempt to make mathematics out of language was futile and the corollary – that if this cannot be done then nothing can be known – bogus. After a couple of months we were still unable to prove to ourselves that the table was not a hallucination, so I abandoned moral sciences for history and pursued my philosophical curiosity alone.

My faith seemed to present me with two things – the first the phenomenon of faith itself, an autonomous method of knowing just as sure as the evidence of my senses or the inference of my reason. Christ the Son of God was a real person with whom I conversed in prayer and joined through the Eucharist.

The second was the more extensive Judaeo-Christian hypothesis concerning God and man. In brief this held that everything is created by a perpetual being whose salient characteristic is love. If he did not love then nothing would exist but he is, as it were, lonely and needs other beings to receive and return his love.

Love by its nature must be voluntarily given so

these beings must be demi-gods who are free to reject him. Like the prince who disguises himself as a pauper to find a girl who will love him for himself, God hides his omnipotence from those he has created. Free will is necessary to make them worthy companions.

First Lucifer and then Adam, under the influence of Lucifer, choose to do wrong. The archetypal man is flawed: the whole race is damned. Whatever the precise nature of the original sin, 'the human race is implicated in some terrible, aboriginal calamity' (Newman) which reduces us to the status of beasts.

God's love, however, persists and looks for a way to exculpate the sinner. What can propitiate God? Who can win him round? Nothing but an aspect of himself – his own love embodied in a son who to reinstate his father's affection must take on human form and be sacrificed like a ram.

There must be some merit in man – some glimmer of faith, some sign that at least one among the many has faith enough to rise above his animal nature and do for God what God must do for man. In obedience to God, Abraham prepares to sacrifice his son. That is enough. His progeny, the Jews, are chosen to preserve faith in a single God throughout the pagan prehistory of man until a sinless woman – an immaculate Mary – appears as an acceptable repository for God made flesh.

Christ is born; preaches; gives ample evidence of his supernatural powers and a clear, unambiguous account of what men and women must do to shed their fallen natures and become, once again, the demi-gods of God's original creation. Before rising to Heaven Christ founds a Church. He appoints leaders with authority to teach, judge and enact the everyday miracle of turning bread into his body and wine into his blood. To one of these leaders – the weak, impulsive but faithful Peter – he delegates his own authority. When Peter is crucified this authority is passed on to a successor, and so on until the Pope of the present day.

How can one prove or disprove such a hypothesis? The supernatural like the aesthetic is not susceptible to scientific tests; indeed any incontrovertible proof would contradict the demands of free will. The only test is to measure it against one's own experience of life. 'For a religion to be true,' wrote Pascal, 'it must have understood our nature. It must have grasped its littleness and its greatness; and the reason for both.' For a novelist in particular it would be impossible to sustain a view of man which contradicted what he observed in himself or his fellow human beings.

In studying the human personality in this respect one is faced with the phenomenon of conscience. Just as an aesthetic sensibility tells us that there is beauty, so a moral sensibility makes us aware of good – not a relative, subjective or conditioned good but an absolute good for all men at all times. 'As we have our initial knowledge of the universe through sense,' wrote Newman, 'so do we in the first instance begin to learn about its Lord and God from conscience.'

If we infer that this sense of right and wrong, implanted in human chromosomes by something superhuman, points to the existence of a Creator; if we surmise like Newman 'that there is a God who cares about what we do, then it is reasonable to suppose that he will try to communicate with us further'. It is also reasonable to suppose that he will communicate with man in a way man can understand

– viz. through language. 'I, Yahweh, speak with directness – I express myself with clarity.'

Now because I have always believed in Christ my knowledge of the sacred texts of other religions – the Upanishads, the Koran, the Book of Mormon – does not equal my familiarity with the Bible: but I have read enough to contradict with some confidence my own father's contention about different religions. The combination of the Old Testament and the New Testament makes the Bible unique. The historicity of Christ together with his character, the subtlety of his teachings and the audacity of his claims are not equalled in the writing of any other religion. If the gospels were works of fiction then, as Rousseau said, 'l'inventeur en serait plus étonnant que les héros'.

Knowing from the experience of a moral sensibility that there is a God, and believing from a reading of the gospels that Jesus Christ is the Son of that God, it is nonetheless possible to reject the particular claims of the Roman Catholic Church. There are, indeed, some contemporary Catholics who appear to regard it as of little importance whether a Christian is a Catholic or not.

It is hard to see how this can be so. If Christ made promises to St Peter and St Peter's successors, and endowed them with certain supernatural powers, it would suggest that Christ thought them necessary or at least useful for salvation. Without authority from above, it is hard to know what is true. The human mind is always interested and fickle, and it is only to be expected that those Christian Churches which are separated from Rome are seen to be built on shifting sand.

The ecumenical spirit requires that we should be

civil to members of other Christian denominations, but our desire for unity must not lead us to accept the lowest common denominator of Christian faith. We cannot proceed upon a pretence that Catholic teachings can be abandoned to accommodate the Protestant conscience. It is difficult, anyway, to identify the Protestant conscience since Protestants appear now to be heretics from habit rather than from conviction. It is hard to find one who believes in predestination, or will say which of Luther's ninety-five theses can be applied to the contemporary Catholic Church. It is hard, too, to find an Anglican to explain how the spirit of God worked through the political compromises in the reign of Elizabeth I; or why a Church governed by a Head of State should seem any less blasphemous and absurd to us now than it did to Thomas More in the sixteenth century.

The only faith other than Catholicism which has ever attracted me was Marxism. As a young man it seemed to me to pursue the concept of charity with an efficacy and vigour which was not evident among Christian societies.

A brief study of history made me realise that, because their paradise must be on this earth, the Marxists pursued it with such savage impatience that most post-revolutionary societies at best resembled Purgatory and at worst Hell.

I also came to realise that Marxism – for all its profession of atheism – depended entirely upon the ethics of Judaism and Christianity and as such was but the last in a series of Christian heresies. Its fundamental premise is that all men are inherently equal and should be treated with justice when in all measurable ways they are patently unequal, and instinctively are as savage as animals in the wild.

The only reason for going against the evidence of one's senses is the word of Christ that we are all equal before God and should treat others as well as we treat ourselves. This Communists mean to do, and in certain places and certain times they have undoubtedly improved the material and cultural condition of men; but their materialistic atheism leads them to poison the soul as they fill the stomach and deprives them of any moral constraints. The end justifies the means and the end is put in a mythic future. To a Christian, as to Camus, the means and the end should be one, for 'what does it profit a man if he gains the whole world and suffers the loss of his soul?'

A more prosaic, rationalist atheism – sometimes called 'humanism' – has never seemed to me to merit serious consideration. 'There are two forms of excess,' says Pascal, 'to exclude reason and to admit nothing but reason.' Rationalists admit nothing but reason yet will not accept what reason itself should tell them – that if there was a being who created man, he would be as incomprehensible to man as man is to an ant. The Christian only suggests that we know something about God because God has chosen to reveal himself. A rationalist may lack faith, but he cannot reasonably deny that a God, if he exists, can provide such a method of knowing.

Pascal invented the computer and dismissed it as a mere bagatelle in comparison to the mysteries of religion. The Victorians developed the steam engine and it went to their head. Faith like superstition seemed an insult to human intelligence and the scientific spirit of the age. Yet few of them had the courage of Nietzsche to throw out Christian ethics with

Christian belief. While proudly asserting their moral self-sufficiency, they lived off the capital of Christianity. Despite modern adherents like A. J. Ayer, this positive atheism of a Marx or a Bertrand Russell now seems somewhat old-fashioned and is rarely to be found.

What has replaced it is a vast agnosticism – not the honest doubt of those who have searched but have not found, but the spiritual indifference of those described by Newman as 'too well inclined to sit at home, instead of stirring themselves to inquire whether a revelation has been given.'

This indifference is perhaps the most unreasonable position of all, 'since it is clear beyond doubt that this life only lasts for a moment, that the state of death is eternal whatever its nature, and therefore that all our actions and thoughts must follow very different paths according to the nature of this eternity' (Pascal).

It is clear, too, that even an agnostic must lead his life according to some system of values – if only for his self-esteem. Most are content to conform to the ethical consensus as reflected in the law of the land; but this has now retreated from its Christian foundations to a kind of benign welfarism which is philosophically absurd. Political pressures lie behind the making of laws in Parliament which are as unlikely to arrive at moral truths as aesthetic ones.

It would be difficult to point to any one moral philosopher whose principles inspire the civic conscience. There is some Marx, some Mill, some Burke and some Bentham. Perhaps the most plausible description of the way people decide what is right and wrong can be found in Adam Smith's *The Theory of Moral Sentiments*. To him morality is based upon sympathy: it is wrong to do to others what one would not want done to oneself.

At first sight such a basis seems reasonable enough – close indeed to the injunction of Christ – but there soon arise victims who are sufficiently different from our legislators, their electors and those who help form their opinions to fall outside the scope of their empathy. Thus the citizen *in utero* may own property – may indeed inherit the Crown itself – but has no right to life. It seems now that the deformed child is expendable while the senile and the insane wait in line. The capital of Christianity is spent.

This brings me back to the phenomenon of conscience and the affront to my moral sensibility of certain acts of others – whether or not they offend the law. It is possible, of course, to suggest that a Catholic only feels revulsion at such legal acts as sodomy and abortion because he has been conditioned by the teachings of his religion; but even an atheist who is indifferent to 'sins' such as these should see the dangers inherent in a system where morality is based solely upon adult sympathy. Where there is no sympathy (or empathy), morality does not apply. There were Germans who thought Jews inhuman, and Bolsheviks who thought the bourgeois were without human rights. Once man makes his own morality anything is possible because man is capable of anything.

I have often observed in testing the Catholic hypothesis that those who live quite contentedly without a faith in God are instinctively decent people. My father was such a man. His faith in humanism was based upon his own righteousness and he would not concede that this righteousness in its turn came from his Christian upbringing.

Towards the end of his life, however, he lost

confidence in the blithe agnosticism he had expressed when younger and looked increasingly not to God but to those philosophers who had believed in God. 'All my life,' he wrote in an essay called *The Cult of Sincerity*, 'I have found more sustenance in the work of those who bear witness to the reality of a living God than in the work of those who deny God – at least the witness of the deniers, Stirner, Marx, Nietzsche, Freud, Shaw, Russell has been outbalanced by the witness of those who affirm God's existence – George Herbert, Pascal, Traherne, Spinoza, Kierkegaard, Hopkins, Simone Weil. In that state of suspense, 'waiting on God', I still live and shall probably die.

'Maybe I have not suffered enough, or been sufficiently conscious of the suffering of others, to need the kind of consolation that a saint such as Simone Weil found in God. Behind every "sincere" belief I detect a special kind of experience which has not come to me.'

In the last years of his life my father suffered very much indeed and perhaps this suffering, at the eleventh hour, led him to God. I myself have never had such 'a special kind of experience' – no dramatic moment of conversion or re-conversion to a faith in God – but I was conscious from quite early in my life of a capacity for evil which by confirming the diabolical made it easier to accept the divine. Novelists, by the nature of their profession, reveal more about themselves than most men; and the facility with which perverse and depraved characters have come to life in my imagination has demonstrated to me my own potential for evil. I am always conscious of the conflict between good and evil within myself; and in the last analysis I believe in God and in the grace of

God because I am not what I might be.

Faith today is made easier by the condition of the Catholic Church. How much harder it must have been for Thomas More to remain loyal to Rome in the era of Pope Alexander VI!

Now, for the first time since Constantine, the Church has disentangled itself from the tentacles of state. No Julien Sorel would today put on the priest's cassock as a cloak for worldly advancement. There is less corruption and more purity of purpose now among the Catholic clergy than at almost any other period in the Church's history.

The very freedom of the Church to pursue its original mission has led to some changes in my life-time. None, I would suggest, are in essentials. The vernacular Mass, communion in both kinds, priests without dog-collars – these are all trivial adjustments when compared to the momentous truths of the religion itself.

There has been a shift of emphasis from prayer and contemplation to good works – a reflection in some areas of the world of the competition for men's souls between Catholics and Communists. There is a less pedantic, legalistic attitude towards sin – more emphasis upon loving than fearing the Lord. Thus the moral behaviour of Catholics may seem less different now to that of those around them. On the other hand those who remain in the Church do not do so for the sake of social conformity but from genuine conviction. With the exception of Ireland and Poland where faith and nationalism mingle together, there are no Catholic countries any more. Nor is there a Catholic culture. There is only Catholic belief.

The contrast between Catholic teaching and the

growing moral chaos in the world at large gives a heroic status to the Church's mission and shows the strength of the rock upon which it is built. The only danger is that confidence in the promise of Christ never to abandon his Church leads one to dismiss the threat from the enemies of the Church. Communism may be discredited in its holy cities of Moscow and Peking, but it remains an appealing ideology to the young and the poor. Islam, too, with its simplistic monotheism and the promise of paradise at a bargain price makes headway in many parts of the world; but neither are perhaps as dangerous as the antagonists within.

For convenience one might describe these as antagonists to the left and antagonists to the right. To the right are the fanatics for the Latin Mass – those who reject all the reforms of the Second Vatican Council because they are aesthetically unpleasing.

The Church, certainly, should be proud of its history and tradition; but it is the Word of God and its meaning which is important – not the sound of it when spoken or sung. To me it is clear that the greater comprehension of the Mass, and the greater participation of the congregation which results, justify the vernacular Mass a hundred times over. I would rather hear and understand the gospel in poor prose spoken with an Irish accent than listen to elegant, archaic and incomprehensible plainchant.

The antagonists to the left are perhaps more insidious because they call themselves 'reformers' and 'progressives', both terms which carry an inherent approbation. They are Protestants in inspiration and like the historic Protestants are commonly found in England, Holland, Germany, Switzerland and North America. They make much of the English concept of 'common sense' and, lacking the imagination to believe in the magical and extraordinary, explain away the supernatural in the Catholic faith with ingenious formulas of obfuscation.

Thus papal infallibility, the real presence of Christ in the Eucharist, the virgin birth, even the resurrection itself are gently laid aside as the improbable exaggerations of a more superstitious age. Like Pascal, 'How I hate all this nonsense, not believing in the Eucharist and that sort of thing. If Christ is God, where is the difficulty?'

Most of their objections seem to stem from the weakness of their faith and their attack is concentrated on the Church's teaching on sexual morality. Many of the issues such as communion for the remarried, the celibacy of the clergy and above all birth control are implicitly a revolt against the Church's traditional mistrust of eros, and their agitation is amplified by their non-Catholic compatriots because more than anything else the Church's strictures on sex defy the indulgent ethic of the age.

It is certainly undeniable that the Church mistrusts the sexual drive in men and women. Apart from the Song of Solomon there is little in either Testament to sanctify or even condone the erotic element in the human personality. Jesus, Mary and Joseph were all celibate and the Church has always prized virginity. The very use of the word 'purity' for the sex-free soul denigrates the act of copulation.

There have been times when this anti-eroticism of the Church has depressed me. Erotic liaisons combined with tender feelings are not just the staple of the novelist's art: they also seem one of the chief joys of God's creation.

It is therefore with some sorrow that I have come

to accept that the Church is right and that novelists are wrong. Art portrays the pleasures of this life, not the next. The whole drift of revealed truth suggests a divine distaste for the erotic. It even seems likely that the aboriginal calamity of original sin was sexual in kind, for why else should Adam and Eve have covered their bodies with fig-leaves? Copulation is undoubtedly man's most animal act. Even as he eats or defecates his mind can be elsewhere, but in copulation body and soul are concentrated in his loins. Orgasm is the surrogate ecstasy peddled by the Devil – an easy pastiche of that mystical state achieved by the most holy saints and ascetics.

This truth about God is hard to accept. We tend to forget that we are made in his image and likeness, not God in ours, and consequently convince ourselves that something so powerful and pleasant must accord with his will. Alas, it is not so, and it would be presumptuous to criticise our Creator for the way things have turned out. 'Is it for you to question me about my children,' asks Yahweh in Isaiah, 'and to dictate to me what my hands should do?' Only in marriage, when sexual intercourse between husband and wife may lead to the propagation of more souls, does God smile on copulation.

The Protestant spirit of the reformers rejects this view which so patently can be gleaned from a reading of scripture. The idea of predestination still inspires them. If the elect make sterile love with a good conscience, then it cannot be a sin. So also if they leave their wives or husbands and marry other men and women.

I myself have no doubt whatsoever that the Church is right in its teaching on sexual morality – even in its teaching on contraception; and if for twenty years I have not practised what is preached it is from the weakness of the flesh, not the commitment of the spirit. I also console my conscience – and perhaps delude it too – that sterile copulation cannot be such a grave sin if it nurtures the bond between a husband and wife, a father and mother.

This view of God's distaste for sex convinces me too that we should retain if we can a celibate clergy. The very virginity of the priests astonishes the unbeliever and attests to their supernatural vocation. The reasons advanced by the reformers for the marriage of priests are always practical – like pushing memoranda from middle-management in a multinational corporation. Priests, it appears, are leaving the Church to marry, and would-be priests are balking at a life without a wife. Yet even on a practical level the Church would need three times as many priests if they were married, because as any paterfamilias can testify family life makes considerable demands and would not only distract the clergy from their mission but tie them into a particular social class.

It is easy to call for heroism in others while showing little oneself. If I was ever to doubt the Catholic faith it would only be because God's gratuitous gift of faith, together with grace gleaned through the sacraments, has not made me a better man. Like the rich man in the gospel, I may hope to keep the commandments, but the prospect of selling all I have and giving to the poor fills me with dismay. The grace of God saves me from the extremes of evil: the weakness of the flesh prevents me from doing much good. My gaze is towards Heaven but my feet are firmly stuck on the ground.

The Things of a Child

LOUIS Mc REDMOND

4

The Things of a Child

LOUIS McREDMOND

I WRITE IN ADVENT. The association of ideas, memories and anticipation which the season conjures to life probably differs little from one to another of us who share the European heritage: bright lights at evening beneath a lowering sky, cheery bustle in the streets, the house filling with the clutter of cards and parcels and kitchen supplies. Dickens did not invent it and it survives, heart-warming, despite the commercialism of the age, especially if children are around. Poverty, of course, affronts the cosy comforts and curdles our happiness a little with guilt. Uneasily, for a moment we wonder whether we merit the joy. For a moment, some might say, Christmas becomes Christian. But that is to moralise and here I want only to describe. I would be slow in any case to suggest that the message has been totally lost. Alms-giving abounds and even the most hardened agnostic knows the story of the ox and the ass, the shepherds, the kings, the child at the centre. Thus Christmas as we have it today, with local variations, from Helsinki to Berlin, to Paris, to London and Dublin.

At one level the picture catches well enough the flavour of Christmas nearly forty years ago in a little country town tucked away in the rolling farmland north of Cork. It had neither department stores nor street-wide illuminations, yet its market square could match the first in raucous jostling while the little shopfronts sparkled as merrily as any confection of fairy-lights. Where Christmas differed in rural Ireland was in the added dimension pervading it, simple to assert but difficult to recreate in print. The sense of coming dominated the town. Sunday sermons and Advent 'devotions', the nuns in their convent school and the Christian Brothers in theirs reinforced the expectation, but these agencies neither imposed nor in any way propagated an attitude which the people did not feel within themselves. Priests, teachers and parents merely articulated what the children best understood, that we were getting ready for the Lord's arrival. Without any diminution of festivities, Christmas Day brought the baby's manifestation amongst us, if not literally, not solely in remembrance either. The sense of incarnation renewed found expression in the several visits made to the crib – originally not an Irish custom, but one well adapted to the Irish mind, to the awareness of Christ-with-us in the here-and-now and of participation somehow, in some way, by us ourselves in the sacred narrative.

I mean none of this mawkishly. We were not an especially pious society. We were no light to a world which, in the war then raging, carried burdens we had not begun to appreciate in our neutral backwater. I say only that we were a believing society. We carried within ourselves a sensitivity towards truths beyond the observable, beyond the comprehensible. We thought it natural that strands should reach into our lives from this reality outside our understanding, and that strands should run from what absorbed us now back to the ultimate truths. This was the wonder of our belief. It involved us. The incomprehensible did not terrify, since it encompassed us, gave us a place and many aids on to which we could latch as links between the finite and infinity. Here was the context of Christmas. Christmas ... unto us a child is born ... a saviour ... salvation. Salvation, the Christian message, the core of our Catholic faith was the concept, the reality bridging the immensity between our daily chores and ultimate destiny. Something particularly Irish marked this emphasis, the folk-memory of a people protected through the long night of tribulation, the lessons cut deep on the Celtic crosses: Moses striking the rock, the children in the fiery furnace, the hand of God stretched out in benison, always the assurance of care and concern and help so that the finite and infinity merged at last in a single reality within which we mortals had our home.

None of us, of course, thought about it like that. It was a matter of how we lived, of what bore in upon our consciousness. It did not make us noticeably good and I am sure we prayed no more often nor more intensely than Christians in secularised surroundings. The fact remained that we dwelt in a two-world dimension where the words of the gospel, the words of the Pope, the words of the politician were equally familiar, equally part of (or equally *not* part of) the communication to which we were open; a dimension where Cana was as actual as the wedding we attended yesterday, where the miracle of the loaves and fishes was virtually as much part of our experience as this morning's breakfast. Christmas illustrates how our worlds merged. I need scarcely add that the phenomenon was not confined to a single season. It was a permanent reality. At Easter we relived the anguish of Calvary, at Corpus Christi Christ-with-us became a theme in its own right as we accompanied the Host in procession and song round the streets of the town. At All Souls we joined with those dead in one world but living in another to affirm the salvation shared by all. Interwoven throughout with this religious awareness was the business of daily living – working, cheating, loving, quarrelling, arguing, suffering, having fun. Faith was not a bonus in our lives like owning a motor-car. It was integral. We possessed our faith as we possessed our inheritance and our beating hearts. And by that faith we were possessed.

It was the deepest and brightest aspect of the Irish Catholicism of the time – a religion which also had its dark corners of anti-intellectualism, narrow-mindedness, authoritarianism, scrupulosity and a tendency to overlap with mythology disguised as history. The defects I concede and I shall talk about them later. In retrospect, they have been much exaggerated. Most Irish Catholics drew pride and comfort from their faith rather than any feeling of oppression. Be that as it may, the way in which religious belief infused and enveloped the lives of the people strikes me still as utterly right. This was faith as it should be, not the arid rationalisation of the academic, not the over-heated emotion of the hot-gospeller, not the privately conserved icon of the sentimentalist's loyalty. It was rather the belief of a believing community, to be lived and lived with. Their natural acceptance made it as credible as the society in which it flourished. God was known through his people. Into this faith I was born; within this faith I grew; the sea-changes of a varied career notwithstanding, to this faith I cleave as a lantern which will safely light me home. Yet, for all my trust, I cannot claim it is enough. A memory vivid down many years, and for no special reason that I can tell, brings me back to a Sunday morning in our parish church. I sat as an acolyte on the altar steps, facing the congregation and the open door through which I saw – I still see – a corner of the market-square smiling in the sun of an early spring. The priest in the pulpit was reading the epistle and I can hear him now: 'When I was a child, I spoke as a child, I understood as a child, I thought as a child. But when I became a man, I put away the things of a child.'

Very recently I visited the town. The church, I found, had been pulled down and totally rebuilt with the exception of the tower and steeple. Inside the new building I stood in the sanctuary and looked down the nave. The exit led into a porch. No longer could the market-square be seen. No longer could the sun be enjoyed from the altar shining on rooftop and house-front. I thought of that Sunday in the distant past and felt that the door had been slammed shut in my face, the vision blocked off deliberately from my view. It was a kind of *déjà vu* because in fact it was many years earlier that the door had been closed on me, bolted and barred. The passively accepted faith with its norms for personal behaviour and its seasonal reminders of salvation history offered too little sustenance in the urban and adult world. Inequality and injustice posed questions, the arbitrary and insensitive exercise of authority by churchmen attracted criticism, conformity clashed with scepticism. For a number, especially the socially concerned and some of the originally uncritical believers, the contrast between what they had known and what they now saw provoked a culture shock which killed off their faith. I am sure they were wrong. I am also sure that they deserve respect for the honest logic by which they allowed themselves to be led in conscience. In Ireland in the fifties and sixties one did not even notice them much. Apart from a very few on the fringes of politics or journalism, they did not advertise their revolt. One heard only after a time that so-and-so was 'not going to Mass'. Upon enquiry it would usually turn out that the errant party could 'not put up with the hypocrisy a day longer'. He or she would have walked away, not rushed to man a barricade.

Those of us – the majority of us – who stayed had no clear motive. It was our contemporaries who 'left' who were expected to have reasons. Retaining the faith might be a matter of profound conviction or of bone laziness, and it might be many things in between. Some, faced with a dilemma such as a Church preaching charity but enforcing draconian requirements on the partners in an unhappy marriage, might say: 'I don't understand these things, but I'm sure the Church knows what it's doing.' Others, the scruple-ridden of whom Ireland was full, would insist that a Church dictate was good and proper *per se* simply because of its provenance: their duty was to accept upon pain of falling through a trap-door into perdition. Yet more, the intelligentsia, reared on Chester-Belloc and contemporary Irish apologists, responded with relish to criticism of the Church by putting together a clever brief for the defence: this always presented Catholic authority as the guardian of truth, a brightly-armoured knight fending off the wiles of a satanic enemy. A few, the most sensible and perhaps the most open to the Spirit's prompting, knew that little was perfect in an imperfect world and were happy to anchor their faith in a Church against which the gates of hell would not prevail, despite its incidental stupidities, pomposities and blindness: Mother Church for them was a loved and loving parent whom they would never disown but who was given to acutely embarrassing behaviour in public, a kindly bumbler. It should be stressed that these and other positions were not so much schools of thought as tendencies. They overlapped and were often found mingled together in adult Irish Catholics. Myriad variations in the blend, from pious asceticism to sceptic ribaldry, gave the local church its vibrancy and savour.

I cannot pretend to identify the precise balance of ingredients from this stock of attitudes which went into my own stance on matters religious. In some degree, I know them all in myself. Otherwise I could not describe them across the divide of many years. I knew two other elements as well. The first was that faith was not for doubting. However inadequate the absolutes of childhood belief, they were neither wrong nor to be discarded. They remained – they still remain for me – the core of faith. They needed to be widened, deepened, qualified, elucidated, added to, if the Catholic Christian was to be girded for a world much more complex than the little town. But this elaboration involved no turnabout. It was merely the digging out of truths unperceived as long as they had not been needed. And if some dilemmas facing the modern Christian seemed unanswerable out of one's faith, this was to be explained by one's own limitations. The answer was buried there somewhere, awaiting discovery. It sounds like an easy escape from uncomfortable confrontation. It would be a mistake, however, to think that problems were rationalised away. Believing genuinely included the belief that answers existed whether they were apparent or not. This was the nature of our Catholic religion. It provided for every situation. If you could see how it did so, well and good. If you could not see, you took it on trust. A pragmatic age may have difficulty in understanding this. It was possible because the faith rested on other foundations than rationality. The feeling of and for mystery was there as well. The mind of God being infinitely greater than the mind of man, it was quite natural not to comprehend everything. Incomprehension was no cause for disbelief.

The second element which I especially recall was that nobody, not even the sceptic, thought to argue within the Church for change. Nobody, or at least nobody whom I knew or read, suggested as believing Catholics that there might be other and better ways of expressing religious commitment – other norms, other prayers, other approaches to the demands of faith. It was not so much that ecumenism was unheard of or the possibility of finding hidden aspects of the truth in non-Catholic Churches; that the shape of the liturgy was assumed to have been fixed for all time; that a married lay-woman ranked three grades below the received standard of excellence (it was never so put, but the assessment could scarely be challenged given the status of the priesthood, of the man in society and politics, of celibacy among the virtues). These phenomena belonged to the static order which prevailed because it dawned on no one to essay a note of dynamism. Only from outside the Church was it urged that the Church might change or be changed, and irish Catholics were little disposed to take advice on questions religious from the lapsed or the Protestant. In any event, the suggestions made tended to be seen as offensive or *parti pris*: the Church should cease to impose its will on civil legislators, on Protestants marrying Catholics, on the life-style of its own adherents. Indeed, it was only from the outside that the Church was seen to impose. To be within was to share the values, to concur in the teaching, to feel at one with the leadership. Commentators consistently failed to recognise this ultimate fact of the old-style Irish Catholicism. It was a Church of the people. Its clergy spoke as its people, from whom the clergy were sprung, expected them to do. Self-questioning just did not arise.

I am tempted to say that this Catholicism of the 1950s, Irish, adult and urban, was no more than a version of the rural and small-town attitudes, a bigger version to accommodate a wider range of experience but essentially the same body of belief. Crablike, the Irish Catholic grew out of his first shell only to fashion himself a greater, more durable and equally snug. If he did, was it so bad a development? Was his consistency to be deplored? Or the attempt to site his earthly life within his faith in the God who saves? Beware of reading yesterday in the light of today's insights. Those who were shown no other cannot be blamed for being wedded to the faith as they knew it. They had many qualities which we may still admire: a strong sense of community, a stoic self-discipline, a commitment to prayer and sacrifice, an urge to draw upon sustaining grace by living to the full what was called 'the life of the Church'. (I wonder how many realise that this is what a high level of 'practice' meant! – a reaching out to fulfilment, not a frightened conformity?) This in turn infused society with an overall decency and order to which it is possible to look back with nostalgia. I, for one, and I hope I belong to the liberal and forward-looking camp, am loath to disparage this older Catholicism. It harboured too much goodness to merit dismissal. Yet, in honesty and disclaiming hindsight, I have to acknowledge that it became increasingly hard to bear its complacency. Perhaps as a lawyer, a journalist and a historian *manqué* I had a surfeit of vantage points. Be that as it may, and despite all the defensive mechanisms available to a Catholic of my generation, I could not avoid the evidence that my religion served less than its divine purpose: my religion, not my faith which certainly was not in doubt.

The situations and events which sat uneasily with my personal religious values, which in turn were rooted in a very traditional Catholic faith, have a clichéed ring about them today. They were the stock-in-trade of the Irish anti-clerical, and for that reason I was reluctant to allow myself to be troubled by them. I could not but wonder, all the same, at the prohibition forbidding Catholics to attend 'the Protestant university' of Trinity College in Dublin. The place was about as Protestant as my own University College was Catholic (I omit the legalisms of charters), which is to say that the religion in most evidence was determined by the composition of the student body. Since Catholics could not go to Trinity, it had a Protestant flavour, and in natural consequence the only other university institution in the city had a Catholic flavour. The Church regulation, which was enforced by the Archbishop of Dublin but, contrary to popular belief, had not been originally decreed by him, seemed to create the situation as much as respond to it. If that was counterproductive, it was surely positively unjust that those Catholics who managed to attend Trinity otherwise than by an act of defiance – and dispensations were not that difficult to acquire – should be refused a chaplain by the Church authorities. It was never explained why this little flock should be left deliberately without a pastor. I could not but conclude that the Church leadership judged it more important to register disapproval than to provide for the cure of souls. The priority jarred with what I had supposed religion to be about.

Other discordant notes in the atmosphere of the time may have been no more than petty annoyances but they set up a toothache nag. The many new churches building in Dublin were grandiose, expensive and aesthetically awful. Where, I asked myself, was the Church of the poor and the patron of the artist? The first question was unworthy. The Church in the relatively impoverished city sponsored massive works of charity – but managed also to let itself down by encouraging profligate philistinism in its outward forms. It was dogmatic also beyond any mandate given it by the Lord. From its constant harping on the 'evils of Communism' to its public support for an indefensible (because undiscriminating) censorship, it presumed to mould a vivacious and imaginative people to the preconceptions of men whose competence as political scientists, as literary critics and even as commonsense citizens was seriously open to dispute. At its worst, this puritan righteousness could warp Christianity itself. When it appeared that the Catholic children of a mixed marriage had been removed by the Protestant parent from their village home in County Wexford to be raised as Protestants, a boycott of Protestant traders in the village received open backing from more than one Catholic bishop. If I never had to suffer in the crucible of doubt, it may well be because Pope John arrived not a moment too soon to give human dignity and the rights of man a higher place than pompous certitude. Here were priorities in which I could concur.

I suppose we shall never be able to recreate the springtide freshness set loose in the Church and the world by the prophetic goodness of the aged Pope. For most of his short reign it was simply a lightness in the air, an encouragement to trust and love and value one another, and especially those whose way of thinking and praying differed from ours. There was more to rejoice about than to deplore, more to share than to reject. These messages of hope reached Ireland and if they did not resolve problems in the field of jurisdiction – Trinity, mixed marriages – they were followed by a speedy and welcome decline in dogmatism. This is not the place to summarise the modern history of the Catholic Church in Ireland. But we all respond to our environment, and it is crucial to my story to record that the Johannine humanity infiltrating our narrow perceptions helped greatly to confirm me in the faith at a time when, it could well be, I might have set off down a different path. I respect those who found solace in the certainties of traditional religion. For myself, I never felt the certainties to be comforting. They were too many and dealt too often with trivia. If they did not contradict the great virtues of charity and justice, as in my examples, they undermined the dedication of one's talents and vision to the service of the Church. Ready-mix religion I found dissatisfying. The truths of faith and the broad principles enunciated by the magisterium within its proper authority were there, as I saw it, for the Catholic to apply in the circumstances of his own life. He retained a discretion in using them, a right to make judgements out of his own ability – and an obligation to acknowledge the goodwill, competence and vision of those of other religious beliefs or none.

What had been an awakening of the spirit, an endorsement of what one felt to be right, became papal teaching with the publication of *Pacem in terris*. I make no general judgement on this encyclical, but I can assert in the most emphatic terms that no statement by a Pope in modern times so moved and enthused me as this paean to liberty, this demand for the recognition of human rights, with the clear implication that the Church could adopt the standards of freedom prevailing in secular society. It made a logical culmination to the pontificate. If the world was by-and-large more good than bad, then it was reasonable to suppose that its painfully evolved political philosophies might merit Christian approval. In fact Pope John went further than merely endorsing individual human rights. He looked back to their origins and their evolution. He used the once-excoriated phrase of the French Revolution, the rights of man. He said that ideas formerly abhorred by the Church might, with historical growth, transpire to harbour wise insights which the Church could make its own. Here, to me, was a perception far more convincing than the dogmatism around me. A Church that could listen and reflect as well as proclaim corresponded to the world in which it had to preach salvation far more closely than a Church supposing itself to have all the answers. Paradoxically, it carried more credibility for me than the cut-and-dried certitudes of what went before. I am, of course, not speaking of revealed truth or the substance of the Credo or the core teaching accumulated down the centuries. I am – I was – contrasting the often insufferable answer-for-everything approach with the style of Pope John; namely, we have good news for you, we want to hear your news, we would like to do

God's work together with you.

The Vatican Council followed. In fact, it had begun before the publication of *Pacem in terris*. It was shot through with Pope John's initiative, even though he died in its first year. Again, I must not use this space to tell a tale which belongs elsewhere. I make two points. First, I eventually found myself in Rome as a newspaper reporter at the Council. This proved to be a further confirmation in the faith. I could speak of the tangible presence of the Spirit. I do not do so because I can scarcely expect others to share my very personal emotion. What I can do is try in a sentence to say why the Council had so profound an effect on one observer. It was because of its human frailty, the groping which it had to undertake to arrive at any decision. Tongues of fire were not to be seen and shafts of light were few – although impressive when they shone. Essentially, we looked upon a body of fallible Christian leaders desperately wanting to lower their anchors in the truth, unsure whether they had found it and willing to speak only when they had heard the many traditions which between them they brought into the *aula*. Yes, if you are thinking it, there were manoeuvres and lobbying and less than edifying pressures brought to bear to influence the outcome on many issues in contention. To me this bore out the presence of the Spirit rather than the absence. I thought it altogether more likely that God should use human beings in their natural imperfection than work solely through saints. We are convinced not only by human reasoning but by human methods of reasoning and of urging a case. At least, so it is for those of us less than saintly. The Council showed the Church to be a human as well as a divine institution, a community for all and not confined to an elect. Here was a Church where you could belong. Here again was credibility.

My second point about the Council is composite. Out of its many teachings, I found a few particularly compelling. The theme that we were each and all the Church, the people of God, took us laity out of a sense of servitude. We were no longer the malleable objects of an authority which might order us about at will. Perhaps I exaggerate the grievance and its resolution. The ordering had been well intended and authority continued intact. What was new was the room created for the laity's contribution to the mind of the Church, and the underlining of authority as service. The faithful and their teacher-leaders alike were thereby raised in dignity as Pope John would have wished. Dignity itself was a concept new as preached, with rights attaching to persons rather than to ideas or beliefs, so that those whom the Church considered to be in error enjoyed precisely the same claim to freedom from coercion as the most orthodox Catholics. This removed any colour of validity from the promotion of injustice in the name of the Church. And man's endeavours through history were judged to have been ennobling, to have made the physical world a better place, to have given cause for joy and hope. This was sane encouragement to give to every man and woman who had troubles enough to bear already and who had one life only each to live. It countered that dark Manichaean inclination to see evil in what cannot immediately be understood. It made happiness in collaborating with God's plan the status quo from which we sometimes deviate instead of an ideal to which we may aspire but are unlikely to attain.

These conciliar emphases put into context the

features of Irish Catholicism which seemed to fly in the face of true religion. The assertiveness, the uncharitable behaviour, the distancing from other Christians: none could survive analysis in the light of the Council. I am not concerned here to ask when such analysis will be taken in hand by the Irish Church authorities in order to eliminate continuing instances of an insupportable attitude. For the unquenchability of faith, it is sufficient that the Church universal has disowned what could not be justified on Christian principle. The application of the lesson may take time – in a human institution, with such a mixture of good and stubborn and pious and opinionated people to be convinced, it must take time. It may be desirable to campaign for the implementation of the Council's vision. So be it. The vision stands, the Church of Christ at the full dimension comprehensible to late-twentieth-century man. In this Church's understanding of itself I see a vindication of the trusting faith of the little town in southern Ireland and the elaboration of what that faith implies for an age and circumstances unimaginable in my childhood.

I could write in more detail, tracing the impact on my faith of journalistic and ecumenical involvement, of reflection on history and politics and social upheaval, of the central importance to it all of the family. But that would have to do with faith as the central stimulus to thought and action. First, it is necessary to have the faith. So why am I still a Catholic? Because the sun still shines upon the market-square.

Reaching into the Silence

BERNARD BERGONZI

5

Reaching into the Silence

BERNARD BERGONZI

I BECAME A CATHOLIC when I was baptised as an infant, sometime in the spring of 1929, in the handsome, Italianate Church of St Saviour in Lewisham, south London. Requiem Masses were said there for my father in July 1969 and my mother in February 1980. I remember it with affection but do not expect to enter it again. To say that I was baptised a Catholic does not explain why I still regard myself as one – there are millions of people in the world who entered the Catholic Church at baptism and who have no visible connection with it any more – but it indicates my origins as a cradle Catholic of mixed Italian and Irish, lower-middle-class and working-class origin; I am not one of those who made the conscious choice of conversion.

My early education was interrupted by periods of ill-health, and by the war, and I never attended a Catholic school. But I read widely if unsystematically in Catholic books and periodicals and educated myself in what now seems to be an extremely rigid form of pre-conciliar Catholicism, which was strong on the need for authority and discipline and very suspicious of private judgement. At the same time I was then, as I am now, a person of liberal rather than authoritarian temperament and when I began to engage in the study of literature I took naturally to the open-mindedness and flexibility of response that literary criticism demands. (A traditional Catholic education did, however, give me a sense of history, and this is something I have always been grateful for.) I suspect that to people who knew me then I may have seemed strangely divided in my attitudes.

In the early fifties the Catholic institution that caused me the greatest difficulty was one that was already something of a dead letter for many Catholics: the Index Librorum Prohibitorum. In principle I accepted that an infallible teaching Church has the right to tell its members what they could or could not read; even if one found it hard to see why a particular book was forbidden, one should accept the ruling in a spirit of disciplined, humble obedience. But as a wide reader of some intellectual curiosity I found the existence of the Index peculiarly onerous; more than that, it was a strange source of mystification, since few people had ever seen a copy or knew for sure what books were on it. Someone with a different temperament would have let well alone, but I was driven by a tormented scrupulosity to discover what books I was not supposed to read. In the Catholic Central Library in Westminster I unearthed a copy of the Index and read it with anxious fascination, picking my way through the Italian of Cardinal Merry del Val's introduction, from which I recall the injunction that no one should complain that the Index represented an interference with freedom, since true freedom lay in following the Church's teachings. I noticed with interest that many of the works on the Index were theological or devotional treatises in Latin from the seventeenth century and that very few books in English were listed. But most of the major nineteenth-century French novelists were there, and some twentieth-century ones; Sartre was added in 1948 and Gide in 1952. Since I was not easy in conscience in reading books that I knew to be on the Index – and since I had acted with what now seems a strange compulsive insistence in finding out what *was* listed – my reading of French literature was somewhat impaired for several years. I pestered the better-educated Catholics of my acquaintance, whether priests or laity, with questions about their attitude to the Index, and discovered that most of them took it much less seriously than I did. Some, of a casuistical turn of mind, said it did not apply to translations, only original works, from which I took some comfort, as possibly enabling me to read Stendhal and Balzac and Gide. Others said that in their judgement the Index had never been promulgated in England, whatever that meant. I wrote to the enquiries column of the *Catholic Herald* and got an unsatisfying answer. Once I attended a Catholic Brains Trust at which a question about the Index was asked; one of the panel members, Richard Stokes M.P., a well-known Catholic public figure and sometime minister in the 1945 Labour government, replied dismissively, expressing mild amusement that anyone should worry about anything so irrelevant and archaic. I was shocked by his flippancy, and my worries persisted. Did the restrictions of the Index apply to me personally or did they not? Had I been a bona fide full-time student the problem would have been less acute, but at that time I was still an autodidact, pursuing my education after working hours in an office job. Full-time students, it seemed, could get permission to read books on the Index if they were prescribed as part of their studies, though even here practice varied in uncertain ways. Some Catholic university chaplains adopted a very liberal attitude, telling their students just to go ahead and read whatever they needed to; but at least one chaplain was said to follow a hard line, requiring a separate application to the vicar-general of the diocese for each book in question; this man must have been regarded as a great nuisance. A few years later I entered university myself as a mature student and by then the problem was not so much solved as dissolved; it had ceased to be an issue for me. Eventually, after the Second Vatican Council, the Index was formally abolished.

I begin with this personal recollection to show what I once was and how far I have come, and I am sure other Catholics of my generation can recall similar experiences, though I believe my particular scrupulous difficulties over the Index may have been unusual. Other young Catholics had problems about love, sex or marriage, but intellectual freedom was a particular obstacle for me. I, and all of my generation who remain in the Church, have come a long way since then. The recent novel by my friend David Lodge, *How Far Can You Go?*, provides a vivid and immensely plausible history of what happened to a representative group of English Catholics between the early fifties and the late seventies. For me, having become a post-conciliar Catholic means, in certain respects, that I am a less divided person. That is to say, the principles of sceptical enquiry, tentative personal response and the avoidance of absolute positions and judgements, which I try to pursue in my professional life as teacher, critic and literary historian, are now central to my life as a Catholic also. At a deeper level, though, divisions and discontinuities persist, as I become more conscious of the paradoxical nature of religious belief, something to be recognised and lived with.

Some cartoons by Max Beerbohm show a writer's young self interrogating his middle-aged self; I wonder what the Catholic I was thirty years ago would think of the Catholic I have become. What, indeed, would he make of the post-conciliar Church, that babble of conflicting voices, where nothing is wholly certain and unquestioned any more? He might react like the publicists of the Catholic right wing, those who contribute to *Christian Order*, for instance, who regard the Second Vatican Council as little short of a disaster (and within their own terms of reference they are clearly right to do so). He might find reassuring evidence of continuity in John Paul II, who teaches much the same doctrine as Pius XII – whom I observed with veneration and awe as he was carried into a public audience in St Peter's in 1953 – and with a similar confident, authoritarian style. Yet the differences are unmistakeable. When Pius XII spoke people took notice, and no one argued back. John Paul II is personally popular, but when he comes out with fiercely traditional pronouncements about contraception or the place of women, Catholics tend to go on thinking and believing and acting in much the same way as they did before. This is true of the laity, at least; priests and members of religious orders – the Dutch hierarchy or the Society of Jesus – have been subjected to very repressive exercises of papal authority.

My young self would be disturbed to discover that Catholicism has been deeply affected by those beliefs that Catholic thinkers used to fulminate against as the pernicious fruits of the Renaissance, the Protestant Reformation, the French Revolution and the deadly onslaught of modern secularism: private judgement, individual responsibility, freedom of conscience, self-awareness and self-direction. He would not be surprised to hear that many Catholics who eagerly adopted these new principles found, in the end, that they could do without the Church and joined an exodus heading for the secular city. He might allege that I, as someone who has remained a Catholic, had little right to the title, since I believed a confused, eclectic mixture of truths and heresies. Explain yourself, he might reasonably ask.

I would be reluctant to do so, for the same reasons that I was initially reluctant to write this essay. My reasons can be summed up in two quotations from Eliot. 'I gotta use words when I talk to you,' says the protagonist of *Sweeney Agonistes*. Statements of belief involve words and attempts at verbal formulation. But as Eliot later wrote in *Burnt Norton*:

> Words strain,
> Crack and sometimes break, under the burden,
> Under the tension, slip, slide, perish,
> Decay with imprecision, will not stay in place...

The older Catholicism never seemed to have worries about words. Everything could be reduced to precise, commanding formulations. One set of words would show that God existed: another that Christ was his only son, who founded a divinely guided and infallible Church, which offered the one sure path to salvation. These lucid propositions were set out in the pages of the catechism, and vigorously proclaimed from the platforms of the Catholic Evidence Guild (which I was on the point of joining as a schoolboy in 1944 until prevented by the start of the flying bomb attacks on London). Everything was so clear and one point followed so logically from another that it was remarkable that everyone in the world did not see the truth and become a Catholic. In the remote past, when people took religious formulations with passionate conviction, men would be burned for a form of words. In my professional life I have learned to take words seriously but with mistrust, following Eliot and Beckett and Wittgenstein; this is one of the paradoxes that sustain whatever religious life I can lay claim to. Formulations like those set out in the Catechism distort the truths they attempt to convey. And yet words are all we have to utter the truth, and ultimately to form our sense of reality.

Religion is about truth and truth is not easily apprehended. Our attempts to define it are partial and deeply affected by the historical and cultural circumstances of their origin. I do not say this as a complete cultural relativist, since that stance is self-defeating and taken far enough would prevent anyone from ever saying anything of interest on any subject at all. Truth exists apart from its formulations, but can only be approached through them. In stressing the historicity of forms of words, and the degree to which they are limited by the mental constructs of their age, needing to be decoded into our own terms if we are to make anything of them, I am closer to the Modernists of the early years of this century than to those who persecuted them. Indeed, the ultra-conservative Catholics who accuse the post-conciliar Church of being 'modernist' are broadly correct (though 'modernist' is itself a slippery formulation). In my youth Modernism was regarded as a particularly pernicious heresy – which had been happily extirpated in good time by St Pius X – and if my young self laid that charge against me it would be a grave one. The nature of knowledge shifts dramatically at intervals in history, and human nature itself changes too; I think that such a shift has affected Catholicism in the past twenty years, shattering the intellectual framework within which I came to maturity, which was drawn from the Scholastic transformations of Aristotelianism, together with elements, particularly in moral rhetoric, of Neo-Platonism and stoicism. For instance, I think it is not an exaggeration to say that an increased understanding of sexuality is leading to a new sense of what human nature is, though this is vehemently and uncomprehendingly resisted in Rome at the moment. The new Catholicism is in the course of coming to terms, almost despite itself, with a twentieth century world view which, in the west, is largely secularist. This is certainly not what John XXIII and the Fathers of Vatican II intended but it is happening: at the same time upholders of the old Catholicism are alive and moderately well and living in Rome. Hence the conflicts within the Church, which I expect to go on throughout my life. I cannot, quite literally, see an end to them and nothing in a mature experience of life should make us too hopeful for a serene resolution.

But Christians are not secularists, despite the facile optimism once expressed by Harvey Cox in *The Secular City*. If the catechism no longer makes much sense to me, I still say the creed, as I did thirty years ago. I say it now as an utterance in religious language, which is also a prayer; I cannot regard it as a series of philosophical propositions, or of historical statements; at the same time, though rich in metaphor, it is more than a poem, a pure literary text; its meanings lie beyond it.

So, *credo*, in transcendence, and in incarnation, mysterious truths, which I prefer to leave in the venerable formulations of the creeds; as a recent religious writer pertinently remarked, doctrine is for many of us best 'left on the back burner'. Accepting transcendence, and being convinced of the importance of institutions, whereby men and women can overcome the limits of individuality and make something together that endures in time and over the generations, one arrives at the idea of a Church, expressing itself in shared forms of belief and worship, with all the paradoxes and contradictions they entail. Once, to be religious meant primarily to be a public adherent of a Church; certainly it seems to me difficult to be religious without some involvement with transindividual forms of faith and liturgy. And yet now, in our society, religious belief is increasingly a matter not just of carrying on inherited, cultural and familial forms and practices, but an individual, existential, lonely act of commitment, which not everyone, whatever their upbringing and background, is able to make. At the same time religion is about transcending individuality, about saving the individual from his apartness. Here is another paradox.

The words of Christ in the gospels are frequently paradoxical, probing, riddling, provoking, more concerned to unsettle than to ratify or to formulate. Yet upon these utterances, so open in their implications, the massive, rigorous, dogmatic, highly organised structure of institutional Christianity has been erected. I am not suggesting that we should get back to the spirit of the early Christians (or abandon institutions in a Quakerish fashion); we cannot, in the late twentieth century, hope to become Christians of the first century; and as human beings we are, I believe, inveterate makers of institutions. But as the history of Christianity shows, it needs constantly to recall the subverting spirit of its founder. Prayer, too, is paradoxical, and not easy for people at home in a secular society (as a pastoral tip to preachers I would suggest that they spend less time telling their congregation to pray, and rather more time telling them *how* to pray). Again, for the most part we pray in words, in the traditional language, worn thin as old coins, of the Church's public prayers. God exists and is to be found, when he can be, in a silence beyond language, but it is only through language that he can be approached.

But still, why Catholicism? I shall risk a formulation, as crude and distorting as anything in the old catechism, but a gesture towards what I believe. Man is a religious creature who needs a transcendent and an immanent God, and a secular age denies this at considerable psychic cost: many people in advanced societies are, as we know, mentally disturbed. The Christian adoption of secularist formulas, such as 'man now come of age', does point to an important part of the truth, but only part of it. Ultimately transcendence and secularism are not fully reconcilable, and choices have to be made. The need for transcendence may be partly satisfied by political and historical causes; a need for immanence, the search for God within, is leading in the west to much trivialising narcissism under the guise of psychotherapy. It is surely significant that Catholicism is growing in Asia and Africa, where religious conceptions of human life remain strong. Perhaps the unimaginable Catholicism of the future will bring together elements from the traditionalism of these continents and the independent-minded, post-secular Catholicism of the west. I believe that Christianity is the highest form of world religion, commemorating in the incarnation the fact that God did in some sense become man, however we choose to formulate that mystery. It has shown itself, however imperfectly, able to transcend its historical origins and speak to all men; and Catholicism seems to me the most visibly universal, in several senses, of the Christian Churches. As an Englishman I am attracted to many things about the Church of England: the beauty of its buildings and its liturgy, the pluralism of its theological life and the absence of dogmatic attempts to regulate the belief and behaviour of its members. Yet the Church of England is based in a fairly narrow segment of English society; so, in other regards, are the Nonconformist Churches. English Catholicism is socially very mixed, and I think this is a source of strength. At Mass a professional man will kneel, or stand, alongside a labourer to receive the Eucharist, an image of true fraternity (or, on occasion, sorority) in a class-divided society.

A few years ago, I was waiting for a plane at O'Hare Airport, Chicago, on a Saturday evening, when an announcement came over the public address system that Mass would be said in the airport chapel, somewhere in the basement. It was not easy to find and Mass was well under way when I got there, attended by a mixed congregation of travellers and airport staff. At the appropriate point in Mass I shook hands with my neighbour, a member of TWA's groundstaff, wearing his overalls; we would not meet again, and would not have much to say to each other if we did, I imagine, but I recall it as a moment of religious and fraternal contact.

I will avoid suggestions of triumphalism. Much of the time I prefer to call myself a Christian in the

Catholic tradition. That tradition, without doubt, means a great deal to me, in the thought, the art, the literature of the west, and it is a matter of some sadness that the Catholic tradition is made so little of in the post-conciliar Church, which is so busy addressing contemporary man that it forgets that the present is formed by the past, and that human identity is nothing without memory; there is an unattractively utilitarian side to contemporary Catholicism. But one cannot impose these things on those for whom they have little meaning. In my youth Catholics accepted authority, while Protestants relied on private judgement; agnostics did not know what to believe. I might define my present position as combining elements of all three: my Catholicism has become quite Protestant, and a reverent agnosticism seems the best response to many of the mysteries or contradictions of existence. There is a sense, too, in which being a Catholic now is like being a Jew, in belonging to a people and a tradition, rather than upholding a particular set of clearly defined doctrines. Such personal ecumenism is, for me, at the moment, a sufficient resting place.

Keeping an Open Mind

CLIFFORD LONGLEY

6

Keeping an Open Mind

CLIFFORD LONGLEY

THE LABEL ROMAN CATHOLIC frankly worries me, for all sorts of reasons. The most obvious is that I happen to have a position as a journalist which would be compromised if it was believed that my writing was partisan. It did not really surprise me in 1972 that certain influential members of the Church of England, seeing that their affairs were in future going to be reported in the country's leading newspaper by a Roman Catholic, reacted distrustfully. And there was another more subtle danger, about which I was warned by an insightful Jesuit at the time of my appointment: that I would actually write more critically and controversially about the Roman Catholic Church than any other. I have, I fear, no real defence against either charge except my own personal commitment to the pursuit of journalistic truth wherever it may lead, without fear or favour.

The second and deeper reason is that I am not even sure it is true. Attached to the label is a set of presumptions and prejudices about the label-wearer's attitudes and beliefs, and indeed for many people that set of presumptions and prejudices is the very definition of a Roman Catholic. But I hold very few of them, in fact. A computer programmed to detect Roman Catholics by posing a series of give-away questions would fail to pin me down as anything at all. The same is true if the definition of a Roman Catholic is assumed to refer to a distinctive moral life-style. I share none of the Roman Catholic Church's attitudes on contraception, divorce, abortion, the religious education of my children, and so on. A religious detective would have to dog my footsteps for a considerable time before discovering a characteristic action of mine which revealed that the label was a correct one, and long before he got that far he would have established to his own satisfaction that I was some sort of eccentric Anglican.

When I read the words 'Roman Catholic' in print I do not mentally substitute the word 'us', a substitution I had once made almost as a matter of course. And so I respond to the statement which is the title of this book with the internal question: 'Am I?' It is something about which I am ambivalent: once intensely so, but more often, nowadays, only mildly, and only when challenged.

My fascination with the issues of religious belief predates any beliefs of my own, and I can remember even as a schoolboy how strongly I had the feeling that religious truth really mattered. I did not share the generally accepted view, even in the fifties, that attitudes in this dimension of oneself were of little relevance to what life was really all about. It seemed an outrage to me, schoolboy prig that I no doubt was, that people should hold beliefs which were incredible and irrational, and that the engines of society – certainly the energies of the educational system – should allow themselves to be used for the perpetration of false beliefs. Militant atheism was my position, and I had the honour to be threatened with expulsion from school for refusing to attend morning assembly, with its low church cant of prayer-hymn-prayer.

I was an adult convert to Roman Catholicism, a person who had the luxury of inspecting Catholicism's credentials rather as one might examine goods in a shop, with no obligation to purchase. It was a dissenter's passage from one form of dissent to another, which seemed at the time to be a repudiation of all I had previously believed, a complete personal revolution. The influences which affected this revolution were complex and subtle, and I would be unlikely to respond to them now. But one must be kind to the person one once was, and the person one once was is entitled to the same respect, including respect for religious belief, that all men deserve at all times.

The experience was first of all one of discovery. I had acquired from my adolescence a certain contempt for the intellectual basis of Christian belief, believing that the whole of reality could be described in terms of scientific principle. Nowhere in my education did I encounter a solid intellectual case for religion, until I stumbled upon the theology of the Roman Catholic Church. There, in what I believe is termed 'natural theology', I came across an exposition of reality from which I found it increasingly difficult to exclude metaphysical reality. The self-sufficiency of science was an illusion: I remember studying at great length a common or garden glass of water, while gradually it dawned on me that there was no adequate explanation in science why it should not that very minute disappear, vanish from the face of the earth. I had, until that moment, believed that the Law of Conservation of Matter guaranteed that no such thing could happen, and any resort to God was redundant. At some instant in time – the memory is still vivid – I knew differently. The Law of Conservation of Matter said only that glasses of water stayed glasses of water however long one looked at them: it had nothing whatever to say as to why this was so. As an explanation it was meaningless; it was simply a description of observed fact. True no doubt ... but neither self-explanatory, nor explained by science. At that moment I became completely dissatisfied with the 'It is so, therefore it must be so' philosophy that had appeared to be perfectly adequate – to me, and to everyone else I knew – and which has never appealed to me again, since that time.

It was also the first occasion on which the concept of intellectual humility had crossed my mind. There was more to truth than I had conceived of, and my youthful conviction that if I didn't know it all I soon would, had to give way to the knowledge that success in the search for truth depended crucially on the spiritual disposition of the seeker. It was at the moment that I had become exasperated with my own stupidity, that I had understood why the glass of water had failed to disappear. From then on, I think, my rush towards Catholicism was headlong: I was hooked.

There is one other experience from that time I cannot dismiss as irrelevant to the present, that took place in the garden (where else?) of a Benedictine abbey. I had retreated there at the suggestion of a priest I knew, who was to baptise me a few days later. It came down upon me suddenly, from nowhere, that I was making a vast mistake. Religious truth was indeed an illusion, and the Roman Catholic Church its principal perpetrator. This – the garden and the concrete bench I was sitting on – was reality, the only reality, the agitated molecules of the sand and cement hitting against my bottom to protect me from gravity; there was nothing other than that, anything else was empty of truth and meaning.

The mood lasted, though I was distracted from it once I came back from the Benedictine quiet to await my four o'clock appointment with the priest at the baptismal font of the local Catholic church. I went through with it, impelled as much by the awkwardness of backing out as anything else, and my principal experience was of self-consciousness,and emotional and intellectual emptiness. The surprise came later, and lasts until this day. It is that I am aware of having inside myself a deep conviction that it was the right thing to do, but more even than that, of a line having been drawn across the page. Not once has the mood of disbelief that visited me in that abbey garden visited me again; and it is as if I am no longer – was no longer, from the moment of baptism – capable of thinking that way. The capacity to have no faith was taken from me. I know of no other experience in my life which in any way resembles it: nor can I explain it, nor do I want to.

I pursued my new faith, for a while, with all the ardour of a convert, albeit one from atheism (which I have discovered is unusual) and albeit to a form of Catholicism which was, at the beginning of the sixties, only just beginning to emerge. My priest-friend-confessor-instructor had come from Anglicanism, and brought a lot of its distinctive ethos with him. His Catholicism, which was the Catholicism I borrowed and made increasingly my own, was the religion of Newman rather than of Pius IX. And Newman, it has been said, was the true father of the Second Vatican Council, whose opening sessions in

Rome more or less coincided with my conversion. Of this connection I was hardly aware, needless to say. It was not why I joined the Roman Catholic Church, though it deeply influenced the sort of member of that Church that I became.

I cannot escape the fact that my religious beliefs have been extensively remoulded by the work I do. It is beholden upon a good journalist to cultivate a certain sort of professional detachment and objectivity towards his subject-matter, to learn to put his private self away from him. There is a kind of discipline to it, absorbed rather than learnt in any formal way. As a court reporter (which I once was) has to pick out from the available information that which is of interest, and balance his report point by point as he describes what he has seen and heard, so a journalist practising in any other field needs to acquire an instinct for balance, and to learn to dismiss his own private opinion from his writing. It is not for a court reporter to play judge and jury, and after a while he finds himself quite agnostic about any particular case. As one very ancient and grumpy chief reporter said, rebuking me as a young man too full of himself: 'The public wants to know what happened, not what you think about it.' It is a fine line to draw, away from the relative simplicities of court cases and local council committees, but it is a valid one. I continue to think that it does not matter what my personal opinion is on some matter on which I have to write; and the habit has become so ingrained that I am very often without any personal opinion at all. This, I may say, is quite unacceptable to some of my readers, who not only insist that I have a personal opinion, but that it must be one that they agree with.

It is not inflicted on very many people that they

have to apply these exacting standards of objectivity to the sphere of religion, the one area where opinion stands out strongly. Almost everyone is committed to something, and has invested his ego in the truth and reasonableness of his position. So might I have done, had it not happened to me that I was appointed to a position on a national newspaper which required me to bring into alignment my religious beliefs and my professional training and experience. I am, I like to tell myself, paid to keep an open mind. In fact, as perhaps only another journalist would fully understand, no other way would be possible. For every day one rehearses both sides of every argument, and holds out to oneself the personal goal that each side must be presented as ably as possible.

One possible solution would be to split oneself in two, being the neutral and detached observer by day and the dedicated man with a cause by night, but the atmosphere of British journalism does not encourage it. What happens, I have observed in others and observe in myself, is that the two halves of oneself come together. The detachment of the professional follows one home; and there are two sides to every question even in the privacy of one's private thoughts. It is not a conditioning I would complain of: on the contrary, I count it a privilege to have been given the chance to acquire such a mental attitude. It has allowed me to get deeper into the heart of religion than I would have otherwise been capable of. More usually, I suspect, those who have burrowed below the surface of religious faith in the search for truths beyond expression have done so by the single-minded pursuit of one single insight. Mine is the opposite way; I have no choice about it; if it does not in fact lead me anywhere, there is nothing much I can do to change it. But I believe, in an open-minded sort of way, that it does ... or might do.

It is true to say, therefore, that I have learnt to be open-minded about many of the questions which Roman Catholicism sets out to answer. And, one hopes, as equally open-minded about rival answers from other brand-named creeds.

It is still almost universally held in the Roman Catholic Church in England today, that that Church and not the Church of England is the true heir and successor of the mediaeval Church of this land; and, needless to say, the opposite opinion is universally held in the Church of England. It could be said to be a distinguishing characteristic of an English Roman Catholic that he takes that view. But I fear I do not know; I hear both sides, could offer a thousand words setting out each case if I had to; but I still do not know, and do not think it ever likely that I shall form an opinion on the matter. It is almost invariably held in the Roman Catholic Church in England today that the Pope has it in his power to define a dogma beyond the possibility of error, and indeed has so defined the dogma of the Assumption. I do not know: I protest I do not know. If you want an opinion, then I think it unlikely, but do not put too much weight on it. And it is the strongly held opinion of the Roman Catholic Church that marriage is, of its nature, indissoluble; that Jesus Christ was the Son of God; that Roman Catholic priests are verily priests, Anglican priests are verily not.

On the first point, my agnosticism is buttressed by a powerful anecdote I heard from a Roman Catholic parish priest, who was embarking upon the unique experiment of a joint Roman Catholic-Church of England parish church. The project had reached the stage of final detail, and the local Roman Catholic bishop visited the building site that was fast becoming a church, to see at first hand. He was shown the baptismal font, and it was explained to him that the parish priest and the vicar had been able to agree on shared use of it.

The bishop thought a little, and then asked the inevitable canon lawyer's question: 'How will we know whether a baby being baptised is being made an Anglican or a Roman Catholic?' The priest, who was practised in both theology and wit, replied: 'We will tie a label round its toe.'

There is only one baptism known to both Churches: each Church recognises the validity of the other's; and the validity of baptism in either Church does not depend on who performs it. Yet the bishop assumed – and who could blame him, for it is what everyone assumes – that there was such a thing as 'Roman Catholic baptism' and 'Church of England baptism', and somehow God could tell the difference. Yet is Roman Catholic font-water any different from Anglican font-water? So what, then, is going on?

The definition of papal infallibility by the First Vatican Council was the high point in the post-Reformation post-Renaissance aggrandisement of the papacy, the point at which the Roman Catholic Church was declared in effect to be a one-man spiritual dictatorship. Was it so in the Middle Ages, and if not, in what sense can the post-infallibility Church be said to be the same as the mediaeval Church? Is not the Anglican Church closer to the mediaeval Church, at least in this important respect? I am inclined to think the answer has to be rather more yes than no. As to infallibility itself, it seems an unlikely thing. My own experience of religious truth is that it is not of the kind that can easily be defined, let alone defined infallibly.

My experience of marriage is that it is not indissoluble. I fail to see how anyone could insist that it is. The traditional indissolublist argument is that once a marriage has been duly and properly commenced then, provided there is no basic flaw such as concealed insanity or impersonation (such as would render it 'not' a real marriage), it will – not should or must, but *does* – last for a lifetime. But what exactly is being said? In what sense can a marriage be described as still in existence when the couple have separated and divorced, and maybe started new families, and maybe lost touch completely?

The Roman Catholic Church, because of its insistence on this theory, refuses to recognise second marriages. But again I do not understand what is being said. That the second marriage does not exist? That is absurd, because it does. That it should not exist? That is at least logical, if impractical. Either way, the divorced and remarried Roman Catholic is an unwelcome guest, not a proper thing at all. And we currently have a pope who takes a far stricter line than the growing if unofficial pastoral practice in England of admitting divorced people to the sacraments. At least he is consistent. But I have to admit that my own experience of being one of the rapidly increasing number of 'divorced Roman Catholics' had brought me to question the legitimacy of the Church's entire matrimonial discipline, and in my own case, to dispense myself from it. It was not difficult, given a year or two's reflection.

I cannot decide upon the meaning of the ordination of men to the priesthood, though the concept of 'priest' is a very powerful and effective one. I prefer to think, from many observations, that 'priest' is a description we all take on at certain times in certain roles, when circumstances demand of us that we should be an instrument of the sacred in our own lives and the lives of others. A priest is one who is empowered to handle sacred things, to mediate between the holy here on earth and the holy that is above, beyond, outside, transcendent. It seems plain to me from the gospels that Jesus meant this to be the vocation of all who heard him. When so much is holy in the world – the Sermon on the Mount points to it, and every single life is touched many times by that strange sermon – I do not see the scope for creating a special class of holiness, the priestly caste, and a special species of holiness, the priestly business of the priestly caste. I cannot therefore choose between the validity of the ordination of a Roman Catholic priest and a Church of England priest, as each seems to be to be a cult-ritual likely to obscure a particularly important part of the gospels. Holiness is all around you, Jesus seemed to be saying; and the Church responded by fencing it off, making it the special business of a few.

And what of Jesus himself? I cannot deny that I would never have taken him seriously as an influence on my own life, without Catholicism. Nor can I deny that it is in that Church, and other Churches, that his most dedicated followers are to be found. In a special way, he 'belongs' to the Church, the institution his followers began to create after his death to keep alive his memory. And I respect very much indeed the dedicated and sometimes unpopular efforts of a special class of his followers, the professional theologians, who struggle to keep that memory alive generation by generation. And from them I have learnt that my own attitude – which is to be very sceptical of any dogmatic attempt to pin Jesus down – is not so unorthodox. Thus I am encouraged to hear Karl Rahner say that the 'is' in the statement 'Jesus is the Son of God' is unlike any other use of the word, and certainly must never be understood as the equivalent of the 'equals' sign in a mathematical equation. This is an even more necessary warning in the case of the statement 'Jesus is God.' As most people understand it, it is not true.

My mention of Rahner, the most distinguished Roman Catholic theologian alive today, is not I hope a sign of some residual party loyalty in me, such as would for example lead me to select a Roman Catholic for mention in preference to the many Anglicans who have written useful things about the issue of the divinity of Christ. It is my experience of such reading of theology from all the major Churches, that Roman Catholic theology at its best is uniquely good, uniquely satisfying. The painstaking integrity of a man like Schillebeeckx in his examination of this famously difficult area is on a par with the very best scientific and literary research anywhere. I fear there is not much Anglican theology about which that can be said. And my feelings are, I know, an echo of that original discovery of the Catholic intellectual mind which caught my imagination more than twenty years ago.

One experience which has grown in me is that the link with my own past I thought I had broken at the time of my conversion is in fact very much alive. My change then seemed a complete repudiation of atheism; what I now prefer to think is that I did not then believe in a God I do not even now believe in, and as soon as I looked in a better direction, there was no mistaking him. There are many Gods offered for our credence, many of them called Christian, and I am inclined not to believe in any of them. They are idols; and the most common idol of all is the God-who-will-fix-it-for-you-if-you-ask-him-nicely. He is the God who is on the side of the powerful, being after all one of them; and the knowledgeable, for the same reason – the father-figure who does not exist.

There is a story told by a German nun about an incident in a Nazi concentration camp, and I tell it with some trepidation as it is not to be cheapened as a mere debating point. The Nazi guards singled out a fourteen-year-old boy for execution, which was to be by slow strangulation in public. The ranks of the Jewish inmates of the camp were ordered to stand in the freezing cold and watch while the boy was hauled slowly up a post by a rope round his neck, there to dangle and kick and die minute by minute before the stunned gaze of family, friends, and strangers. One of the Jews begins to mutter, blasphemously cursing God and denying his existence with increasing anger until he turns to a rabbi in the row nearby and demands: 'Where is your God? What use are your prayers? Look at that!' And the rabbi replied to him: 'There is God; hanging from the post.' And with that protester, I am an atheist; with that rabbi, I also believe in that God, hanging.

The memory of Jesus is important to me in understanding the story, and I am not uncomfortable with his pathetic cry of 'My God, my God, why hast thou forsaken me?' It is a cry which beckons me on, which feeds my desire to come closer to the heart of religion. But I am not fussy about sources, and some of the best little nuggets of gold I have found mixed in the sand of my sifting tray have strictly non-Christian origins.

For several years I found myself locked out of non-Christian religion, unable to pass through each particular gateway and yet perceiving that there was truth to be had on the other side. I became aware, for instance, that many Jewish friends made much of the same sort of criticisms of the Christianity they saw around them as I did, and they complained about the same kind of distortions of the truth as I did. Although all the language was different, I sensed a kind of recognition, a familiarity, as one might detect the voice of a friend in the hubbub of a crowd.

At the same time I began to read of mysticism, as publishers followed the fashion towards Eastern religion. I read a Roman Catholic nun writing: 'Christianity is mystical or it is nothing' and an Islamic professor using almost exactly the same words about Islam. A friend turned my attention towards the Sufi poetry of Islam, and again there was that sense of familiarity dressed up in slightly unfamiliar garb; a book review, and then the book itself, brought me to have another look at Zen (by which I had been baffled on first encounter). I did not, I think, ever even begin to pull up my roots in Christianity and plant myself elsewhere, but my gradual education in this esoteric world of mysticism caused me to think quite deeply about the nature of Christianity. It seemed that I may have missed the point – not by a long way, but far enough to make me dissatisfied. It made me, I must confess, totally impatient with the paraphernalia of Catholicism, reinforcing other trends in my life at the same time.

Even so, I was reminded many times that I was not the only person in or near the Catholic Church who had such second thoughts, and who found the preoccupations of the 'official Church' and 'official Catholics' in the Church hard to share. I know that for many older Catholics the changes of the Second Vatican Council and what has happened since have been about as much as they can really cope with, and they are inclined endlessly to relive the great victories and defeats of the sixties. This is as true of the so-called 'progressives' as of the 'conservatives' – but meanwhile water is still flowing under the bridge, and the issues have moved downstream. I could indeed myself once be called a progressive Roman Catholic; but the feeling has grown in me that it is all a game, that the old issues are no longer central. I am no longer upset by the Sacred Congregation for the Doctrine of the Faith – let them do what they wish. I have somehow managed to move myself beyond their reach. Clerical politics! What nonsense it is!

The tragedy is that I am not the only one who knows it, but I am the only one allowed to say it. Invited to give an address to a congress in Brussels, I chose to say exactly what I thought, rather in the spirit of this essay now, and to confront them for once with the crushing irrelevance of so much that preoccupies the 'professional Christian'. I argued, for instance, that the Church is not a 'real' community at all; and yet so much of modern theology begs this very vital question. I had mixed feelings about attending the congress, even more so as I was to be a key speaker, and felt that my reputation as a 'Roman Catholic journalist' was rather bogus. Perhaps for once, away from home, away from 'the readers' (that strange corps no *Times* journalist ever forgets), I could let my hair down, say what I thought, deliver my swan-song as a 'Roman Catholic journalist' and walk away free.

But they liked it, and many of them agreed with it.

I had a letter from a very senior Roman Catholic African clergyman, who had been at the conference, telling me how valuable it had been, and how he was still thinking over what I had said. How glad he was that someone had said it! And I have had other instances of the same thing: for some reason people will confide in journalists, and I hear many things I cannot write about. And I hear echoes of my own position, in the most surprising places.

What it amounts to is this. I (we?) do not any longer look towards the Roman Catholic Church or any other as a supernatural society, and cannot in all honesty put my name to whatever might be officially described as 'the teaching of the Roman Catholic Church', I do not accept its jurisdiction over my private life; would not dream of going anywhere near the confessional; go to Mass very little; and do not worry about it. Yet I would not finally repudiate it, and if they introduced a simple ceremony for leaving it I would not take part. I would not join any other Church, towards which I would feel an equal or even greater lack of empathy. I do not like the style, yet I am very fond of the people. And I feel very at home with them: some of the finest people I know have committed their lives, but not *to* the Church, *through* the Church, to the advancement of the welfare of their fellow men. And in the lives of those I know really well, invariably there has been some crucial experience in which holiness, the sacred, has been mediated to them by someone whose presence at that point was occasioned by the Church, possibly even by the official ministry of the Church, but sometimes quite unofficially and probably against the rules. Such people who have been touched in this way by the transcendent God usually have a right sense of perspective, and regard the doings of churchmen, popes or otherwise, as not what it is all about. I find them talking not about being 'good Catholics' – that death-dealing phrase – but about being human, and how to advance the humanisation of their fellows. There are of course many such people outside the Roman Catholic Church, and I have ceased to regard this as either paradoxical or important. There could be times when every single person of this quality is unable to identify anything good in organised Christianity; there could be times when the Church is committed to dehumanisation, and has to be opposed root and branch. I have lost any ability or desire to distinguish between Catholic and non-Catholic, Christian and non-Christian, or any desire to be counted on the one side or the other: but on the side of truth, wherever it breaks out.

These categories are, I believe, of far more importance to the clergy than to the laity, who are used to making a wide variety of personal relationships with all sorts of people without even taking religious labels into the reckoning. And one cannot be unaware of the fact that some of the finest people I know wear no religious label at all, and some of the most insufferable wear their religion on their sleeves. It seems to be generally true that a great many of the details of 'religious' activity are given a significance out of all proportion by those who have a vested interest, who are almost invariably clerics. They have, of course, dominated the religious life of this country since time immemorial, and in the past their definition of what was important was generally followed by opinion at large. I cannot ignore the fact, however, that very large numbers of people continue to regard themselves as 'religious', in some relatively undefined but sincere and significant respect, but virtually dismiss the entire domain of 'clerical' religion as having no bearing on their lives at all. I have felt my own attitudes evolving in this direction too. And I do not think it would be healthy if the large number of people who think religion is important were to start taking the clergy too seriously. It cannot be emphasized too much that an issue is not necessarily important because one clergyman, or indeed a whole consensus of clergymen, says it is.

Further, I believe that the Roman Catholic Church is an institution which is not only dominated by clerics, but defined by them. Thus one is tempted to understand the question: 'Am I a Roman Catholic?' as meaning in fact: 'Do the clergy regard me as one?' And the test, which I must say strikes me as laughable, tends to centre round such clergy-orientated matters as the observance of obligatory Mass attendance, regular confession, marriage according to the rules, sending one's children to schools approved of by the clergy, and so on.

And yet I am also aware that there are many enlightened clergy who would agree with the general tone of these objections of mine, and whose response (like mine) is to dismiss 'ecclesiastical' definitions and look at the heart of the matter.

And I take seriously what I hear when I hear them say that in their eyes, notwithstanding the vagueness and looseness with which I take this business of denominational labels, I am 'one of them'.

What I think they mean, which is the only sense in which I can endorse the title of this book, is that 'being a Roman Catholic' is not necessarily – or essentially – a matter of categorising people according to certain criteria of ritual behaviour ... Mass, confession, marriage in church, and so on. It is not in the same class of definition as one's nationality, sex, height, colour of eyes. It is not really a personal description at all, nor is it about membership of a distinct group, though that is how the concept has been used in the past. It is about where one turns for inspiration, where one's source is, which wavelength one is on. Catholicism is not something I belong to, in the sense one might belong to the local Save the Children Fund committee. Catholicism is a well one draws from, as for example classical music is a well one draws from. Told by somebody that classical music was an important source of meaning and inspiration in his life, one would not naturally reply: 'Ah, then you are a classical musician'. It is not that sort of thing. It is not about labels at all.

And if I say that some of the insights into how to live life that have come to me have come from reading Islamic poetry or staying with a Zen koan long enough to peel off some of its layers, I would not, I suppose, automatically be categorised as a Moslem or a Buddhist. That is how it is with me and Catholicism too, except that to date Catholicism has had more influence than any other source of spiritual wisdom. Therefore I respect it very deeply. And it will mean other things to other people, including those to whom it is important that 'Roman Catholic' should be a badge they wear round their neck. I can respect them, knowing that they are putting it to different use, and that we are all at different stages. For them it is part of identity, to me it is a source; but for them it is not the whole of their identity, nor is it my only source.

There are very many people who, according to the 'clericalist' definition of the term, are no longer

Roman Catholics. They have found the institution wanting in some important respect; in many of them there burns a deep anger and hurt, a sense of having been led towards a certain destination and then let down when it really mattered. For them gradual detachment from institutional Catholicism was not an option: they did not stay with it long enough to carve out for themselves a new and more productive way of relating to it. Such people have rarely been granted an insight into what I would like to think of as the true heart of Catholicism – a heart not so far removed from the heart of Islam, Judaism, or indeed Buddhism, though that last reference must be subject to many qualifications. That, I am sure, is Catholicism's failure, not theirs; though it is their loss. And the 'clericalist' definition of a Roman Catholic is so powerful and pervasive that any attempt to maintain an alternative is met with incredulity.

That alternative exists and is valid and effective, and I think we shall hear much more of it. The statistics of religious affiliation in England have shown a surprising trend in recent years, indicating that there is now a substantial element in the population who do not completely repudiate their Catholic origins, but who have ceased to observe the norms of Church religion. Once it was not so; either a Catholic went regularly to Mass, or ceased to call himself a Catholic at all. But the statistics show a large and growing number – which I think is still a substantial underestimate – of those who are Catholic in the sense that many Anglicans are Anglican. And in particular they repudiate the rules of the game, defy the clericalist definition.

It started with the birth control crisis in the sixties, and it is given new impetus by the divorce crisis in the seventies and eighties. It is an inarticulate movement, unled and not theologised about. It is not – and this is a striking fact – a problem to itself; it is a problem only in the eyes of the clergy, for very many such people are quite comfortable where they are, and not looking for somewhere else to go to.

I am not sure I would count myself among them, an alternative group to identify with or an alternative label to wear. In the great majority of cases, the distinctive Catholic-ness about them comes from the formative period of their lives, their family life (with Catholic parents and brothers and sisters) and their schooling. I do not have that in common with them: their state of spiritual equilibrium must be different from mine. In particular, there must be considerable conditioning and guilt to come to terms with, sensations I do not feel. I identify much better with someone like Simone Weil, the 'Red Virgin' of pre-war France, and in particular with her difficulties over taking the step of becoming a Catholic. She died unreconciled to the Church, though according to my own use of the term she was one of the most remarkable Catholics of the century.

Simone Weil stopped just one step short, on the far side of the technical boundary the Roman Catholic Church draws round itself, and my own condition could be compared to a mirror image of hers. I would not take the final step out that she would not take in, and I think our reasons are not so different; though in no other way would I want there to be a comparison between myself and such a remarkable woman. But we are both in our own ways citizens of the same boundary country, and her example at least tells me it is not a barren country. Peasants who live close to national frontiers tend to make light of those frontiers, and customs posts and border guards are for those who live right inside or right outside, not for those from the border lands. If we live with the best of both worlds, we also live with uncertainty, not always quite sure which side of the line we happen to be on at any one time, and not always quite sure where our loyalties lie. It requires a particular temperament, perhaps: I am the last person to suggest that my own position is the only true one, or to urge the rest of mankind to come and join me.

Giving Birth to the Future

JAMES P. MACKEY

7

Giving Birth to the Future

JAMES P. MACKEY

THE IRISH PLAYWRIGHT Brendan Behan, when asked once about his religious persuasion, declared himself to be a bad Catholic. But he added immediately, in case any of his hearers should think that a note of contrition could be detected in his voice, that this was, of course, the only thing to be. The statement, as one might expect from the man, was a perceptive one. It was certainly not a simple-minded expression of that kind of Catholic chauvinism which believes that even a bad Catholic is better than a good anything else.

There is a great deal of truth in Roman Catholicism, and so much that is right about it, but it has the ability and the habit of making to seem bad any who deviate from its relatively comprehensive and relatively rigid norms. It is not, of course, the only social grouping to have this ability or to indulge this habit. There are Christian groups in both East and West that would make Roman intolerance look like a flabby and unprincipled liberalism. But there is within the Roman Catholic version of Christianity a perspective upon Christian truth that makes its institutional intolerance much less defensible.

Roman Catholicism depends upon its deviants, as much as other Churches do, for a dynamic future, and one presumes that a dynamic future is what all Roman Catholics desire. Fossils survive longest, but at the cost of no longer living. Their forms retain the memory of past movement, and a quick glance at them can sometimes glean the impression that they still live. But they are no more than the solidified *rigor mortis* of the past, and a deadly warning to those who do still live that they had better keep moving. Now there is within Roman Catholicism a perspective upon Christian truth which gives a particular impulse to movement outward and onward – the kind of movement outward that is not colonial and the kind of movement onward that does not foreclose upon the future – and it is to this more than to any other single factor about it that I would personally point if asked for justifying reasons for my continuing commitment to the Roman Catholic Church, such as it is.

And yet, if I am to maintain any modicum of honesty, it is not with this kind of consideration that I ought to begin. The reasons why any of us are anything in particular, the reasons why we are *still* something or other, have more to do with wombs than any of us would normally be prepared to admit. I am a Roman Catholic from my mother's womb, and that soapy phrase 'our holy mother, the Church' means more to me than any normal adult male chauvinist should be expected to admit. On Sundays I go with my family to a Latin Mass at the cathedral in Edinburgh and I feel security wafted towards me like warm air from the familiar clipped Latin phrases of the congregation's recitation of the *Gloria* and the creed, and a cooler and more distant sense of security coming down from the altar where the priest recites the old Latin canon, invoking the past through its popes and martyrs and saints, and calling for the ghostly presence around us of all the living and the dead as the drama of the upper room, the root symbol of God's definitive act of grace in human history, is re-presented. When my seven-year-old daughter complains that she doesn't want to go to *that* Mass any more because she does not understand what 'they' are saying, I know that she must soon have her way, and that I must not exploit at her tender age her willingness to learn Latin. Yet I feel the frustration of all good conservatives before peremptory demands for change. But, more than that, I find myself reflecting upon the fact, and I'm sure it is a fact, that authoritarian prohibitions of older practices can be just as much an abuse of authority as are preventions of progress towards renewal. They can represent a futile effort to hide the fact of change, change which is always advertised by the coexistence of the old and the new. Consequently, they can represent the wish to cling to an absolute form of authority long after models of immutable truth which alone support such forms of authority have begun to disappear. Few ways of tinkering with the truth can be more dangerous than to act as if any form of its expression which human beings possess is absolute, immutable or wholly irreplaceable.

In any case, apart altogether from the clamour and the questioning of the young already born, wombs in the natural course of events exercise their own pressure on those who prefer the warm darkness to the blinding light, the encompassing waters to the work of creation. And, sure enough, there have been in my generation's experience of Roman Catholicism pressures which would push us out to positions we have not yet fully dared to occupy or for that matter (for here is the paradox of motherhood) been allowed to occupy.

Since the Eucharist is the whole of Christian faith

and life in sacramental form it can continue to illustrate this theme. The pressure for more frequent communion at Mass was there from my youth, but it really began to succeed only when the vernacular liturgy made participation in general appear more obvious. (And the vernacular liturgy in turn was part of a more general movement – in theology too – to put the people more in possession of their faith and to have it seem less and less the preserve of Church officers.) Actions, like the mother pushing out her child, often have implications that are unknown at the time and seldom altogether welcomed. The negative effect of increasing communion was a major decline in confessions, but its positive effect was to make the Eucharist a little more like what in essence it is, a meal. This did not, of course, decide the old, misconceived theological problem as to whether the Eucharist is a sacrifice or a meal. But, if it had been taken far enough, or if it had been allowed to go far enough, it would have shown in practice that the eucharistic meal is itself sacrifice in sacramental form.

That last phrase is not meant to mystify anyone. On the contrary, its meaning is simple. To break bread and to share a cup round the table of the Lord Jesus is to signify effectively that one gives, as Jesus gave, whatever is required for love of another, even life itself, and that one does this for enemy as well as friend. Or, since all sacrament really has petitionary form, one prays through the Eucharistic action that one may do as much. So, as the Eucharist becomes more a meal, its sacrificial nature emerges all the more strongly, and it needs no mystifying theological theories on how an ancient execution can be made present again at a different point in history. But then, of course, we try to reverse the natural direction of the movement in part, and in part we are held back. Few of us in private or political life follow the logic of the sacrament to the point at which it requires us to make sufficient sacrifice that the starving of the world should eat and that those found in the prison of oppression should be free. And we Roman Catholics in particular have closed our Eucharistic table more to our fellow Christians than they have to us or to each other, despite all the theological agreement on real presence already achieved. Jesus is not really present where even fellow-Christians refuse to break bread round his table, and no theological theory ancient or modern can make him present in such circumstances. It is a sobering fact that our much-vaunted documents of Vatican II do not at any point envisage the future union of Christians except in terms of the return of all separated brethren to Rome; and it is a sad fact that this rigid view is ruining our Eucharist. Will the move towards more communion ever reach full Christian maturity? It will, of course. It is already doing so, at the risk of some daring, and some downright disobedience.

Problems in Eucharistic theory and practice are closely bound to problems of ministry, and here also Rome has recently made moves the full implications of which are not always seen or, if they are seen, are strongly resisted. There can be no doubt whatever that when Rome in the sixties began to dispense what were misnamed 'laicisations' this represented to me, and I'm sure to many, many others, a push towards that option. Undoubtedly our holy mother, the Church, was herself under some pressure, but, just as certainly, her reaction to the pressure put some pressure on her offspring. All births are like that; and it would be the height of irresponsibility for either mother or child to wish to deny its part in the new emergency (from the verb 'to emerge'). I do not wish to comment at any length here on some of the more sinister forms of irresponsibility shown by Church officials towards the new breed of married priests. These ranged from a rather pathetic propaganda which talked about secular priests breaking a vow of celibacy (which in fact they do not take), or talking about reducing them to the lay state (laicisation which in official Roman Catholic theory cannot be done), to downright immoral efforts at giving them an immoral reputation (an appalling travesty of that pastoral duty which is the sole *raison d'être* for any office in the Church). This is particularly dirty Roman Catholic linen and should not, except in cases of extreme provocation, be washed in public.

There may, however, come a time, and it may be soon, when some of those who have trifled with the moral reputations of married priests may have to be faced in public with the contrast between men who struggled honestly if sometimes unsuccessfully with their sexuality in human relationships and those of their would-be judges whose pastoral record was pathetic, or whose own sexual behaviour was less honest or more private or transformed into even more questionable desires for power or position or even for what one Irish writer called the grosser materialism of the belly. The moral blackmail exercised by some Catholic leaders in cases of 'laicisation', as they call it, simply has to stop. As I say this, I must add that I was not subjected to it during my own process.

Neither do I wish to comment on the various kinds

of irresponsibility – ranging from indifference to the Church to outright hostility – in which those of us who have 'left the priesthood', as our action is again erroneously described, have sometimes engaged. The Roman Catholic Church now has in fact thousands of married priests, of whom I am one, and, though almost all of them are in a state of forced pastoral inactivity, it is upon the positive prospects of this recent Roman Catholic event that I wish to comment. For I believe it was a happy event essentially.

By allowing so many of its priests to marry the Roman Catholic Church has shown in practice that marriage and priesthood are compatible. Its concomitant decision to forbid its married priests to function as such, except in the most extreme circumstances, simply illustrates by its disciplinary nature the purely 'positive' legal nature of that separation of priesthood and marriage, which was not decreed by the founder, but is a product of Christian history. In short, what the Church has *done*, more than anything it has said on these subjects, presses towards the abolition of a priestly caste and, of more importance, towards a true acknowledgement of the equality of the married state with any state of life possible for a Christian. The ideal of celibacy will be secure, indeed it will be enhanced by freeing it from the strictures of legal imposition on all members of a particular vocational class. Celibacy, which Catholics are wont to confuse with virginity, refers to the unmarried state and, like most negatives, it needs a positive prospect which positively requires it to make it part of a moral ideal. There are and always will be Christian projects of prayer and praxis which will require that men and women, priests and laity go without the founding of their own families in faith, love and hope, and these will always find men and women, priests and laity, who will exhibit the corresponding types of faith, love and hope of which Christians are capable. But it is surely silly to suppose that every priest in a parish or a school is asked for those kinds of self-sacrificing love which require celibacy, and it is surely sensible to suggest that those who are not called by choice or circumstance to projects requiring those kinds of self-sacrificing love are better off learning that other kind which is taught in the spiritual school of Christian marriage.

Once again the pressure is there for Roman Catholic movement outward and onward, though once again it is resisted. It is a matter of mixed joy and sorrow to me that my ordination to the Christian ministry is acknowledged – and acknowledged in practice, where acknowledgement counts, in invitations to preach – by the members and leaders of Churches other than my own. But what is acknowledged by my fellow Christians is *my Roman Catholic priesthood*, and therein lies the inspiration for me and, I would hope, the example for my fellow Roman Catholics. For what is revealed here is a crying need for the Roman Catholic Church, through its officers and leaders, to take full responsibility for what it has been doing for so many years now and on such a large scale: full pastoral responsibility towards those priests who think themselves too late or otherwise unable to marry, and who are bitter that if some have been allowed to do so they too should have been long ago allowed; full pastoral responsibility towards those priests who have been allowed to marry but who have been told in so many unsubtle ways to go hide themselves somewhere or other; full pastoral responsibility towards those whose applications for permission to marry have been quite unjustifiably delayed; and above all full pastoral responsibility towards those members of the Church, whether future priests or future married priests, who will see the implications of what the Church has done, whether it be officially admitted or not.

Here, then, is just another example of combination of movement and inertia, pressure and resistance to it, which characterises Roman Catholicism today. But it would not be right to leave this example without noting that a particularly sinister form of resistance to the natural momentum of allowing priests who wish to do so to marry may be in preparation. The usually reliable sources have it that Rome is now contemplating a manner of dealing with requests from priests for permission to marry much as it deals with many requests for the annulment of marriages, i.e. by attempting to ascertain if the priest was somehow 'unfit' for priesthood at the time of ordination – by retrojection, of course, of more recent behaviour patterns. This, if there is any truth in the rumour, would be a step backwards of such destructive potential that it might make one regret that the step forward had ever been taken. It would repeat the fiction of so many marriage cases – seen to be necessary in order to maintain the questionable distinction in those cases between nullifying a marriage and declaring it to have been null – that partners who are now incompatible were originally so.

More seriously, it would weaken the only defensible theology of priestly vocation as consisting supremely in the call of the Church; it would exacerbate the tendency to see priests or those who 'stay in the priesthood' as being *eo ipso* more worthy than others (which they blatantly are not); or it would make marriage and priesthood incompatible in a way which no part of Church doctrine other than its positive law ever thought them to be, and this, as ever, to the detriment of the married state; or all of the above. And where would it leave me, and thousands like me, who have not been given, and might well not have accepted, permission to marry on such conditions? It would certainly confine the incidence of married priests in recent centuries of Roman Catholic history to our lifetime, but it would also be the most abject refusal of responsibility on the Church's part for what it has recently done and a pre-emption of the positive possibilities of what it has done, such that it behoves all married priests to do all in their power to prevent it.

But that, surely, is a laughable phrase, if ever there was one. Married priests in the Catholic Church doing all in their power? Married priests with power? In the Roman Catholic Church? Yes, it is slightly laughable, I suppose. Although, if laughter is to be a criterion, it is no more inherently humorous than the sight of some poor men in the clerical hierarchy wielding feudal titles ('my Lord') which little in their social background had prepared them to hear, and which nothing in the scriptural norms for leadership in the fellowship of Jesus could in the least support. The only model of leadership which the founder of Christianity could tolerate was, paradoxically, the slave model, so that authority exercised in the Roman Catholic Church on any other model can be safely ignored – with safety to one's Christian integrity at any rate, although, depending on one's position or function in the Church, one's vocational safety might not be at all guaranteed.

However, viewed from outside the range of laughter (be it healthy, sarcastic, or hollow) patterns of power have been changing recently in the Roman Catholic Church. It is true that the changes have been noticeable in the conduct of persons in high office, whereas the official documents of the Church still describe the power of its offices in the legal language of legislative, judicial, and coercive power which fits states more than Christian communities and ancient empires more than modern states: good Pope John showed us what the Pope's proudest title – servant of the servants of God – could mean in practice, while the Second Vatican Council still described his office in terms taken from and fit only for an ancient Roman Emperor. Again the surge of new life breaking old forms and the restricting contractions, the rhythm of birth. Pope John XXIII has had no equal in this century, though our present leader seems determined to give body to an image of the Pope as pastor of the world; and that remarkable concern for the dignity of humankind, and more particularly for the wretched of the earth, which characterises all his missionary journeys could yet do as much as anything that John did to render obsolete the secular legal model of authority in the Roman Catholic Church which is still written into its constitutional law, and which no one as yet seems to have the prophetic vision or confidence to remove.

This quality of concern for the human gives a lead that the Church badly needs if the full truth of the belief that God became flesh is ever to be truly perceived and persuasively preached. The Roman Catholic Church in some countries is still too insular or, in countries where it holds a minority, too much victim of its own ghetto mentality, to be able to echo this human concern and add to it. Yet one must be heartened by the recent meeting of the National Conference of Catholic Bishops in the U.S.A. in its prophetic resistance to its government's false propaganda and inhuman policies towards countries in Latin America, and in its approach to the view that to be pro-life is to be against nuclear arms, and to be against nuclear arms is to be against war as such. The Roman Catholic Church's contribution to the workers' freedom movement in Poland needs no comment from me – though I notice that Leszek Kolakowski in a recent article in *The Times Higher Education Supplement* could describe this 'first workers revolution' with no more than one passing reference to the Church. (Even Reformed Marxists can find it difficult to be honest about religion.) Roman Catholic communities as extensive as the nations they inhabit may yet, under such leadership, arrive at the deepest Christian conviction that all life is grace, that all grace is a gift to be given again, and that to die in this conviction, rather than threaten to kill for lack of it, is the consummation of that indestructible joy which this conviction alone can give, though only when it is a lived conviction rather than a doctrine held captive in the mind.

Reference to doctrine in a paragraph on the Pope inevitably brings before the mind that image of the present Pope which depicts him as human and progressive in external affairs but a hardline conservative in matters internal to the Church itself. Even those who accept this image sometimes defend it on the grounds that a Pope who is so concerned with the plight of people under dictatorships Christian or Communist can hardly be expected to have much patience with the pampered Catholics of Europe and America when their women demand more and easier contraceptives, their priests clamour for permission to marry, and their theologians insist upon ever greater academic freedom in dealing with received doctrinal formulae.

It is to the last point, on the Pope's attitude to theology and theologians, that the question which forms the title of this book might be expected to draw my particular attention. But not exclusively, I hope, if only because even Roman Catholic theologians are also members of the human race and some, like myself, are actually husbands and fathers. So I feel entitled to remark, first, that the ambivalence of the Pope's office already mentioned – described in the legal terms of empire while being exercised in the pastoral mode – compromises the efficacy of the missionary journeys: the one who pleads for human dignity has to sit down to a state dinner with a Roman Catholic dictator in the Philippines. Secondly, for the Pope to align his authority with a distinction between such fluid terms as natural and artificial in the case of contraception is not just an academic mistake to which theologians might be expected to point. It represents an unwillingness to listen to such representative bodies as the 1980 National Pastoral Congress at Liverpool: a conference notable, surely, for its balance of loyal commitment and equally loyal and constructive criticism, and as clear a contrast as one could wish to the 1980 Synod of Bishops with its deliberate hand-picking of lay representatives on grounds of their known allegiance to *Humanae vitae*. However, the Pope is a travelling pastor. And he will come to England and Scotland, and if he cares to listen he will hear the married Catholics' witness. Or, to put the point in the language of Roman Catholic piety: unless our holy father the Pope and our holy mother the Church are to develop into some kind of androgynous monster, the former must listen to the latter with as much respect as he expects to be heard. Finally, the distinction between external affairs and internal matters is not as well established as it might seem either to those who use it to defend the Pope or to those who use it to attack him. For if the Catholic Church's case presented by its leader is based upon a truly Catholic perspective it will apply equally to those inside and outside, wherever that dividing line is drawn. Before looking to that perspective, mentioned at the outset of this piece and as a means of coming closer to it, a few words about the Catholic theologian in the Church would seem to be in order.

On the one hand academic theology has a quite minor contribution to make to the Christian life. The essence of Christianity lies in orthopraxis rather than orthodoxy. Like any other way of life it has its own means of propagating itself and its survival is not dependent upon the contribution of the academic analyst and his or her scholarly critique. On the other hand mind control – the control of what people think, or think they know or believe – is one of the most effective methods of control, as those who have been most successful in achieving and maintaining positions of power and privilege have always known. Theology, therefore, whose immediate subject matter is systems of belief, in its practice provides a particularly apt illustration of that movement of expansion and contraction so characteristic of contemporary Roman Catholicism, and in its theory it should be able to point up that theme of a perspective on Christianity which makes restrictions upon its movement less justified than they might otherwise seem, a theme with which I began and with which I hope to finish.

1968, the publication of *Humanae vitae*, provided a watershed for Roman Catholic theology and a crisis for many of our lives. By complete contrast with the encyclical of similar sounding title of some two decades earlier, *Humani generis*, it provoked a critical reaction from theologians that was without precedent in this or in recent centuries. But the theological reaction, by focusing too soon on political issues of authority rather than pastoral issues of family life, made theologians to seem – and this was our own fault – rivals for the kind of authority which then, as now, Roman Catholic constitutional law attributed to the hierarchy alone. Theologians missed the opportunity of displaying a different, more Christian understanding of authority, by concentrating on the pastoral issues of the morality of the family and offering their Christian analyses of these as *service* pure and simple to the other members of the Church whether clerical or lay.

Then, when priests were allowed to marry and many theologians were amongst the first to do so, Rome tried to make sure that such married theologians did not teach in Catholic seminaries or Catholic faculties of theology. The theological resistance to Roman autocracy, however, was by now well established and many Catholic institutions of higher learning ignored these directives, quite rightly. And yet many of those who by pressure or choice moved to non-Roman Catholic faculties of theology found a new freedom and a new confidence in their Roman Catholicism which they might never otherwise have found – because they discovered simultaneously the true Catholicity of their version of the Christian faith and, almost of necessity now, the servant model according to which they should conduct its dissemination. Though I was myself under no pressure whatever to leave the Catholic University of San Francisco after I married, the confidence in their own tradition which the Presbyterians at Edinburgh University showed in the ecumenical gesture of offering me one of their traditional chairs proved to me the value of what I possessed, a value of which those who fear to open themselves to the other or the new have presumably never appreciated.

As soon as Roman Catholic theologians stopped worrying about authority and got on with their job they began in fact where all true Christian rebirth must begin. They began with Christology and have by now given an example to other Churches on the method and content of such necessary renewal. Not that they have been allowed to forget the issue of authority. Two of the most influential and creative Roman Catholic theologians, Küng and Schillebeeckx, have recently been under investigation, and the document from the Congregation for the Doctrine of the Faith which tried, by *fiat*, to prevent Küng from being what he is, namely, a Roman Catholic theologian, proved that the necessary change in the understanding of power and authority in this Church, to bring it more in line with the power made perfect in weakness and the paradoxical authority of the slave, is still a long way off in some quarters. For the document is characterised by an obsession with teaching authority and infallibility (arguably, apart from its political use in supporting certain claims to a certain kind of authority, the most useless doctrine ever 'defined' by any Christian body), even to the point of, first, claiming for the civil servants of that Congregation a role in safeguarding and promoting the doctrine of faith and morals in the universal Church (a classic example of creeping infallibility) and, second, of actually suggesting that errors in other doctrines which it mentions, significantly, only in passing, are to be attributed to lack of respect for this teaching authority so understood. The document also mentions Hasler, a priest whom that Congregation unsuccessfully tried to have laicised by his bishop for his published views on infallibility – is there a better way than this of showing contempt for the Church's own doctrine of priestly ordination? – and whose deathbed letter to the Pope would, if it were known more widely, stand as one of the monuments to conscience in this otherwise undistinguished age.

There are, of course, significant connections between certain views of authority, infallibility, over-emphasis on doctrine in Christian life, its alleged immutability, Christian ministry, its decreed celibacy, inertia or intransigence on some moral issues, and eucharistic theory and practice. But only a sustained theological analysis of book length could do justice to these. I have subsumed them all under my by now undoubtedly over-used image of birth, with its pushing out and yet wishing to retain; being pushed and going out and yet wanting to remain within. For I do believe that in our time, more than in the recent past, my Church is in fact giving birth to its own future and, foolhardy or not, I see in what others call the conservative backlash simply an essential part of the rhythm of this movement. I am not, as many preceding remarks must have shown, unaware of the un-Christian and indeed inhuman actions and attitudes that are too often taken or taken up in the course of this difficult exodus, of the intolerance so often shown on all sides – and, no doubt, in this essay also.

But even here I would point in hope to that Roman Catholic perspective on Christian truth which, like the best wine, I have kept until the end.

Early in its history and by a combination of historical influences which are by their nature accidental, Christian theology began to develop a cluster of largely coincidental distinctions between, for example, reason and faith, nature and grace (or supernature), creation and redemption. After the sixteenth century those branches of the Christian Church in the world which considered themselves Reformed tended to harden these distinctions into contrasts, whereas the Roman Catholics, as they now unfortunately had to be called, insisted upon some kind of continuity across the distinctions. The distinctions themselves should never have been allowed a permanent place in Christian theology because, whatever temporary advantages they might confer in the course of particular polemics against outsiders, they serve in fact to hide from view the deepest truth about Jesus of Nazareth and about the faith which he brought into the world. It is a truth not easy to express, practically impossible to live, yet essential to try to grasp for all who would be called Christian. One of its most intriguing expressions in recent times took the form of Bonhoeffer's unfinished speculation about the prospect for a religionless Christianity.

If religion be defined, as it surely must be, as a matter of formalised creed and moral code, cult and societal constitution, then it is well to remember and salutary to recall that the religion of Jesus himself was the Jewish religion of his day and none other. It is the faith of Jesus, which found its first expression in that religion, that is definitive for us. And at the centre of that faith there were, to imitate Marx's phrase about 'relations of production', relations of grace, the lived relationships to one's own life and to all people and things as God's unconditional grace or gift, by which alone the fatherhood of God, in Jesus' sense of that common symbol, was to be encountered. That lived faith has been embodied since in many complex forms of religion which have developed from each other or been differentiated from each other in the course of Christian history, of which the modern Roman Catholic form to which I belong is but one, though an extremely large, powerful and, I believe, vital one.

But it is the relations of grace that make Christianity, its inner essence as well as its historic goal. With respect to these the various forms of religion, as defined above, are symbol or sacrament: the Churches are sacraments; the Eucharist, obviously, is a sacrament whose light is refracted through the rich profusion of other sacraments in the Church; the creeds or doctrinal summaries are, according to their ancient name, symbols. But when these signs effect the reality which they signify – the definition of a sacrament on which I was reared – the signs themselves will wither away.

Then, since all creatures great and small in the relations of grace mediate to us the fatherhood of God and since the Christian religion in all its forms is the symbol or sacrament which at once participates in and tries to effect this reality, there is no distinction between nature and grace. The best that I can say for the Roman Catholic tradition, but this I can say for it, is that although it too operates with this distinction, its sense of the continuity between nature and grace will lead one, by the inner logic of this sense, to the dissolution of the distinction between them. And, as it does this, it must make one more open to all the world as it groans for freedom and fulfilment, more tolerant of religious forms past or in the process of being born, less authoritarian in the name of either office or vocation. This perspective on Christian truth I learned from my Roman Catholic tradition, from its theology of nature and grace, from its sacramental theology and above all from its modern Christology, and to this I look whenever the intolerance of vested interests in the Church, whether it comes from bishops acting as lords, or theologians acting as oracles, or lay people hiding their responsibility under profuse protestations of loyalty to holy fathers or holy mothers, makes the slow progress from symbol to reality more painful than joyous, and even more hazardous than in the nature of things it needs to be.

As I began with an Irish writer, I might as well end with one. Brian Moore's novel *Catholics*, which I encountered as a TV play in America, was rightly seen by most people as a satire on Roman antics in the change over from the old liturgy to the new. But to the central character in that play, the abbot, the problem was the ability to believe at all, and not the problem of the forms, ancient or modern, Latin or English, in which that faith might be embodied. His faltering effort to say the 'Our Father' was the true climax of the play and showed it to have depths unexpected at first sight. And in that scene the drama of our modern age, perhaps of every age, is crystallised. No Christian can wring some drops of hope out of the tragedy of threatened faith who does not refuse the idolatry of his own ecclesiastical forms. But neither has he anything to contribute except what these passing forms have carried down to him, safe so far from the ravages of time.

Books Referred to in the Text

Cox, Harvey *The Secular City* Penguin edition, 1968

Küng; Hans *The Council and Reunion* Sheed and Ward, 1961

On Being a Christian Collins/Fount 1978

Does God Exist? Collins, 1980

Lodge, David *The British Museum is Falling Down* Panther edition, 1969

How Far Can You Go? Secker and Warburg, 1980

Moore, Brian, *Catholics* Cape, 1972

O'Malley, Mary, *Once A Catholic* Amber Lane Productions, 1978

Read, Sir Herbert *The Cult of Sincerity* Faber and Faber, 1969

Smith, Adam *The Theory of Moral Sentiments* edited by Raphael, David Daiches and Macfie, Oxford University Press, 1976

Williams, H. A. *The True Wilderness* Collins/Fount 1976.

Biographical Notes

Robert Nowell is a journalist specialising in religious affairs. Born in 1931, he became a Catholic while an undergraduate at Brasenose College, Oxford. He was assistant editor of *The Tablet* from 1962 to 1967, and editor of *Herder Correspondence* from 1968 to 1970. Since 1970 he has been a freelance journalist. He is the author of *A Passion for Truth: Hans Küng – A Biography* (Collins 1981). He is married with four Children.

Mary Craig combines being a housewife with being a broadcasting journalist, lecturer and author. She was born in 1928 at St Helens in Lancashire and studied Medieval and Modern Languages at Oxford. She is the author of two best-selling books *Blessings* and *Man From a Far Country* (both published by Hodder and Stoughton). She is married with three sons.

Piers Paul Read is the author of eight novels and two works of non-fiction. Born in 1941, he was educated at Ampleforth and St John's College, Cambridge. His novel *Monk Dawson* won the Hawthornden Prize and the Somerset Maugham award. He is married with four children.

Louis McRedmond has written and broadcast on Church affairs for many years. He is a barrister by profession and a historian by training, but long ago became a journalist by choice. He was a reporter at the Vatican Council and has been Dublin correspondent of *The Tablet* since 1966. Since 1973 he has been Head of Information in RTE, the Irish Broadcasting Service. He is married with four children.

Bernard Bergonzi read English at Wadham College, Oxford, and began his academic career at Manchester University. He is a Professor of English and currently also a Pro-Vice-Chancellor at the University of Warwick. He is the author of several books of literary criticism, including studies of Hopkins, Eliot and the modern novel. His first novel, *The Roman Persuasion* published in 1981, is about English Catholic life in the 1930s. He is married, with a son and two daughters.

Clifford Longley has been religious affairs correspondent of *The Times* since 1972. He has acted as adviser to various radio and television programmes including Thames Television's award-winning documentary on Cardinal Hume. As well as covering current events in his field in *The Times*, he contributes a weekly column published every Monday. He has three children and is married to an American.

James P. Mackey has been Thomas Chalmers Professor of Theology in the University of Edinburgh since 1979. Previously he was Professor of Philosophical and Systematic Theology in the University of San Francisco. He has been associate editor of *Herder Correspondence, Concilium,* and *Horizons*. He has published many books including *The Modern Theology of Tradition* (Darton, Longman and Todd), *Jesus, The Man and the Myth* (SCM Press) and *Tradition and Change in the Church* (Gill and Macmillan). He is married, with two children.

Also available in Fount Paperbacks

Christology
DIETRICH BONHOEFFER

'The publication of Dietrich Bonhoeffer's *Christology* in English is an exciting event, for here we are given at last not only the basis for his thinking about Christ but the key to his whole theology.'

T. F. Torrance, Scotsman

No Rusty Swords
DIETRICH BONHOEFFER

'Anyone who would really know the man who wrote the *Letters and Papers from Prison* must first follow the struggles and development of the young Bonhoeffer outlined in this book.'

Times Educational Supplement

The Way to Freedom
DIETRICH BONHOEFFER

'Readers of *No Rusty Swords*, the first volume in this trilogy of collected letters, lectures and notes of Dietrich Bonhoeffer, will need no persuasion to follow this inside story of one of the key figures of twentieth-century Christianity.'

Scotsman

Bonhoeffer: An Illustrated Introduction
EBERHARD BETHGE

'. . . will introduce Bonhoeffer to a new generation of readers, giving as it does a vivid picture of the young theologian's life during the rise of Nazism.'

The Friend